The Weapon of Choice

Despatches from the front line of
an adult eating disorder unit

SOPHIA PURCELL

To Mum,

I'm sorry for what you're about to read, but I
hope you'll be proud of how far I've come.

Never again will a single story be told
as though it's the only one.
– John Berger

Enjoy your body. Use it every way you can. Don't be afraid of it, or what other people think of it. It is the greatest instrument you'll ever own. Dance. Even if you have nowhere to do it but in your own living room. Read the directions, even if you don't follow them. And don't read beauty magazines. They will only make you feel ugly.

– Baz Lurhman

Grant me the serenity to accept the
things I cannot change,
The courage to change the things I can
And the wisdom to know the difference
– Serenity prayer

You have nothing to prove to anybody.
You alone are enough.
– Maya Angelou

Contents

Prologue

This book is based on my experience as an inpatient on two separate acute adult Specialist Eating Disorder Units (SEDUs) for patients with anorexia nervosa, between 2021 and 2022. All those mentioned have given full consent to be included, but some names and details have been changed to protect the privacy of both patients and staff.

Although on the whole, this book is about eating disorders, it is not about eating or not eating, and most of all, it is not about food. As I always say, food is just my brain's weapon of choice; a way to cope when everything feels like chaos, and I have nowhere to turn, and paradoxically, not a choice at all. Of course, food is mentioned, but really and truly, it is just background noise. More than anything, this book is about what it's like to have an eating disorder, and most importantly, what happens when you try to live without it.

I first developed anorexia as a teenager, and although I always knew it had a big impact on me, I never dreamed I would still be struggling as I entered my thirties. So, what I've written is as much about anorexia as it is about my life; about what it's like trying to muddle your way through adulthood with a brain that, ultimately, wants to kill you.

I want to stress that what follows is an account of my own personal experience of living with, and undergoing treatment for, anorexia nervosa - an illness I have suffered with for over 13 years. Although my experience is not unique, it is perhaps a little different from the 'norm' - whatever that may be. This is because I not only have anorexia, but also cerebral palsy, a physical disability that affects my balance, muscle tension, flexibility, coordination, and general range of movement.

In writing this, my intention is never to upset or offend anyone, but I think it's inevitable that some parts of my story may be triggering; especially to those who are caught in the cruel grips of an eating disorder themselves. There will be no mention of numbers, calorie counts, behaviours, or any other talk of that kind, but if you think you're not in the best place to read this sort of story, please, please quit while you're ahead, keep yourself safe, and reach out for some help. The UK's eating disorder charity, Beat, has some really great support, so they're always a good place to start, and I've included their details in the resources section at the back of this book.

The 14 and a half months I spent as an inpatient saved my life; there is no doubt about that. But I will always look back on this period as the time I learned that it was possible to break your own heart. So, if I have one hope for what I've written, it is that some people may be able to relate to my story, and that maybe, just maybe, it might inspire them to continue striving for a life beyond their eating disorder.

Index

This isn't really an index. It's more like a list of words and phrases you probably won't have heard unless you've had the terrible misfortune to find yourself in an inpatient Eating Disorder Unit.

Anorexia / Anorexia Nervosa (AN)

Anorexia nervosa is an eating disorder that is usually - but not always - centred around restricting food and / drink to influence your body size, weight and shape. It can also involve other behaviours such as excessive exercise, laxative abuse, and self-induced vomiting.

Avoidant Restrictive Food Intake Disorder (ARFID)

Avoidant Restrictive Food Intake Disorder or ARFID is an eating disorder that is characterised by a person avoiding certain foods or certain types of food, having a restrictive intake in terms of the amount of food consumed, or all of the above. The reasons behind these behaviours can vary, but having to eat food a person would usually avoid can cause high levels of distress.

Behaviours

Behaviours are routines or rituals around food that are common among people with eating disorders e.g. cutting food up into very small pieces, eating foods in a certain order, only using specific plates / cutlery, mushing food up, over using condiments, taking food apart, or only eating certain foods. The list is by no means exhaustive, and all these types of behaviours are banned in eating disorder units.

Body dysmorphia / Body dysmorhic disorder (BDD)

Body dysmorphia is a mental health condition where a person sees themselves in a way that does not reflect how they actually look (e.g. seeing themselves as being larger than they actually are), and spends a lot of time worrying about perceived flaws in their appearance.

Binge / Bingeing

When a person consumes a lot of food, usually in a short space of time, even though they are not physically hungry.

Binge-eating disorder (BED)

Binge-eating disorder is a mental health condition where a person feels compelled to over eat on a regular basis, doing so when they are not physically hungry, and until they are uncomfortably full.

BMI

This stands for 'Body Mass Index' and it is calculated by taking a person's weight in kilograms and dividing it by their height in centimetres squared. Developed in the 1830s by a male mathematician, it's complete and utter bollocks, but unfortunately, it's still used as the main way to determine who gets help for their eating disorder and who doesn't.

Bolus

This refers to the process of being given nutritional supplement (fortisip) through a Naso-gastric (NG) tube via a syringe. And yes, it really is as unpleasant as it sounds.

Bulimia

Bulimia is a mental health condition characterised by regular, secretive periods of over-eating, followed by self-induced vomiting or other compensatory behaviours such as laxative abuse or excessive exercise.

Care Plan

A document that outlines a patient's assessed needs and how they will be addressed. Usually, a care plan is divided into sections called 'Keeping Safe', Keeping Healthy', Keeping Well', and Keeping Connected.'

Care Programme Approach (CPA)

A meeting held every 5-6 weeks to discuss a patient's progress and plan next steps for treatment. Usually, all members of the hospital MDT are present, as well as the community support team e.g. Eating Disorder Nurse / Practitioner, Care-coordinator, and any family members where relevant.

Care Quality Commission (CQC)

The CQC is the independent regulator for hospitals and social care settings in the UK, and basically, they're the ones who decide whether or not a facility is doing its job properly.

Eating Disorder

I feel as though I'm stating the obvious here, but it's got to be done. Although this will likely mean something different for everyone, an eating disorder is the name given for a range of mental health conditions in which there is an ongoing disturbance of eating behaviour that has a significant impact on a person's life and wellbeing.

Eating Disorder Practitioner (EDP)

An eating disorder specialist who is in charge of a

patient's care within the community i.e. when they are discharged from hospital.

EDU / SEDU

This stands for Eating Disorder Unit or Specialist Eating Disorder Unit. Basically, a ward within a psychiatric hospital designed to treat patients with eating disorders. In this case, specifically Anorexia Nervosa.

Formal

If you are admitted to hospital on a Section 3, or detained under the Mental Health Act after being admitted, you are classed as a 'formal' patient. This means that if you try to leave the hospital without permission, the police will be called and you will be brought back. This also affects your rights as a patient, and means that if necessary, you can be given treatment against your will, if it is deemed to be in your best interests.

Fortisip

A nutritionally complete supplement drink used in Eating Disorder Units as a meal replacement. It comes in various flavours (banana, vanilla, chocolate, strawberry, tropical, raspberry etc.), all of which are equally vile.

Feed

A nutritionally complete liquid formula that is administered on an hourly basis via a pump and an Naso-gastric tube.

Flush

After a Naso-gastric feed is finished, the tube needs to be flushed with water via a syringe to ensure it doesn't get blocked. This is known as getting a 'flush.'

Health Care Assistant (HCA)

Although not generally medically trained, these make up a large proportion of the staff. They provide support, advice and assist with the day to day running of everything, and without them the ward would be on its knees.

Informal

This refers to patients who are admitted to hospital on a voluntary basis, i.e. of their own free will as opposed to being detained under the Mental Health Act. This is a bit of a catch-22, because many patients end up agreeing to go into hospital informally, only to avoid being sectioned. As an informal patient, you can refuse treatment and discharge yourself from hospital unless your responsible clinician (e.g. a consultant psychiatrist) feels there is a significant risk to your mental and / physical health.

Multi-disciplinary Team (MDT)

In an EDU, this usually consists of a GP, a consultant psychiatrist, a dietitian, an occupational therapist, a nurse, and a psychologist. Essentially, all the professionals who are in charge of every patient's care.

Mental Health Act / Mental Health Act Assessment (MHA/ MHAA)

This is the process by which a person can be detained in hospital under a section, usually when they refuse to go to hospital for treatment, or try to leave once they are already there. In either case, if the MDT decide that it is not safe for them to be out of hospital, the responsible clinician (usually a psychiatrist) can apply to a court for them to be detained under the Mental Health Act 1983. Once a person has been placed under section, they may be given treatment against their will (such as Naso-gastric (NG) feeding).

Naso-gastric feeding (NG)

This is the means by which a patient is given nutrition via a tube that goes through the nose, down the throat and directly into the stomach. This is usually done when a person refuses, or is unable to maintain an oral diet.

Obs

In an EDU, patients are required to have their vital signs, or 'obs' checked at least once per day, depending on their physical health risks, and how long they have been in hospital. This usually includes oxygen levels, pulse, blood sugars, and sitting and standing blood pressure.

Occupational Therapist (OT)

An occupational therapist provides 1:1 and group support, aimed at making the time on the ward more enjoyable, and helping patients to develop the skills needed to cope safely and independently at home.

Orthorexia

This is a type of eating disorder that involves being obsessively preoccupied with only eating foods that are considered to be healthy or 'clean', and can also include exercise behaviours as well as a need to control weight or maintain a certain body size / shape.

Purge / Purging

This is a compensatory behaviour aimed at reducing, losing, or controlling weight, either by self-induced vomiting, laxative abuse, or excessive exercise.

Replacement

A nutritionally complete supplement drink (e.g. Fortisip, Ensure, Fresubin) that is used as a meal replacement. If a patient does not finish a meal, whatever is left will be calculated and given to them as a replacement. Usually, patients are given a 10 minute time limit to finish this, before it is noted down as a refusal.

Restraint

If a patient is detained under a section 2 or 3, they may be given treatment against their will. This can sometimes result in a restraint, whereby the person is held down and forcibly fed via an NG tube, and as you can imagine, it is not very pleasant for anyone involved. Restraints may also occur to prevent patients from trying to abscond, or cause harm either to themselves or another person.

Safe foods

Safe foods are exactly what you'd expect: foods that feel 'safe' to eat and therefore don't cause as much post-mealtime guilt as other foods might. These can be anything and vary greatly from person to person, depending on their eating disorder and individual preference.

Section / Sectioned

This refers to the process by which a person can be detained in hospital under the Mental Health Act 1983, either for their own safety, for the safety of others, or both.

Section 17

When a person is sectioned and detained in hospital under the Mental Health Act, their responsible clinician (e.g. a psychiatrist) can grant them a leave of absence from hospital under Section 17. This can be anything from a matter of hours to a matter of days, dependent on risk.

Supervision

A period of time - usually 1 hour / 30 minutes - after meals and snacks, during which patients must sit without moving, fidgeting or engaging in any compensatory behaviours. This should always be supervised by a member of staff, hence why it's called 'supervision.'

Ward trip

A ward trip is exactly what it sounds like: time away from the unit as a group to do a recreational activity e.g. bowling, going to the cinema, pottery painting.

Ward Round

A weekly meeting involving a patient and members of the MDT. The purpose of the meeting is to discuss the patient's progress, and for the patient themselves to discuss any issues or concerns they may have about their treatment.

Water loading

A behaviour whereby a person consumes large amounts of water / liquid before being weighed to influence the number on the scales.

Chapter 1
The Bottom of The Well

A few summers ago, I spent the afternoon in a park watching a small group of people celebrating a family birthday. They had balloons, party food, cake, cards and presents all spread out on a picnic blanket, and every so often, would cheer with delight as they popped open bottle after bottle of prosecco.

I, on the other hand, had just split up with my long-term boyfriend, lost my job for the third time in as many years, and Covid-19 was just beginning to wreak havoc across the world. And to top it all off, I was deep in the throes of anorexia.

Sitting on the grass surrounded by pigeons (which, I discovered, are actually quite beautiful if you take the time to notice them), I was on the phone to a psychologist from my local eating disorder service.

She asked me - as she did every week - how I was doing, and I replied - as I did every week - that I was fine: *actually, honestly, in spite of it all, really, completely and utterly fine.* A statement which both of us knew was complete and utter bollocks.

Once the pleasantries - and bollocks - were out of the way, I said:

"I don't know. I just feel like I'm at the bottom of a well."

"Okay..." she started, clearly not sure where this was going.

"I feel as though, without ever really knowing it, I've fallen down a well and I can't get out. So, now I'm just here and it's dark and cold and I keep trying to climb back out again, but...I dunno. I can't. You keep asking me how I'm doing and what I'm eating and giving me suggestions and trying to help, and I've just been going round in circles, slipping further and further down this well. I'm trying to get a grip on something - anything - but it's like there's nothing to hold on to. The walls are all slimy and...I'm stuck."

"Right, okay. That makes sense," she says.

"Does it? I ask.

"Yeah, it's a good analogy. It makes total sense," she tells me, a little too enthusiastically.

"What can you see?" she asks.

"What do you mean?" I say.

"From where you are. In the well. What can you see?"

"Er...nothing. I can't see anything. It's just black."

"What about if you look up? Can you see anything then?" She asks again, her questions gathering momentum.

"No, I still can't see anything. It's all just really, really dark."

"Okay, but you *know* there's a top, don't you? You know there's light at the top of the well, even though it's dark, because that's how you got down there."

"I guess so....?" I say hesitantly, beginning to lose any concept of where this might be leading.

"So, we just need to find a way to get you back out again. You said there's nothing to hold on to, but there is. You just need someone to be at the top, holding out some rope for you to grab onto, to pull you out again," she says, her tone of voice both reassuring and yet somehow defiant.

"Right," I say, hating how sceptical I sound.

"Think of it like...do you remember that story about those miners in Chile? It was in the news a while ago. They were stuck underground for days and days and everyone had started to give up hope, but they were rescued in the end - all of them."

"Yeah, I remember," I tell her, laughing in spite of myself. "Are you comparing me to a Chilean miner?"

"Well, no, all I'm saying is...I know you feel stuck, and that's understandable - I get it. But you're not going to stay stuck. You just need someone to be there at the top, lowering down a rope to help you out, and that's what we'll do. That's what I'll do. It's what I'm here for."

* * *

A couple of months later, it is the middle of winter, and I am alone in my flat, wearing layer upon layer of clothing but still feeling frozen to the bone.

Outside, the air is crisp, and the sun is streaming in through the windows, casting delicate shadows across the living room floor.

I open my laptop to start a Zoom call, already knowing exactly what I'm going to say.

The call begins, we both smile and wave, and she looks at me and asks - as she does every week - how I'm doing.

Instead of saying *"I'm fine - totally, completely and utterly fine"*, I say:

"Do you remember that time in the summer when I told you I felt like I was at the bottom of a well?" I ask.

"Yes, I do," she says, her words slow and deliberate.

"Well, this morning, I...I went to brush my teeth and...I just couldn't do it," I mumble, trying as hard as I can to get out what I need to say.

"Okay," she replies gently, her words half acknowledgement, half question.

"I just couldn't do it, because all I could think about was how many calories there were in toothpaste." In that moment I laugh, just as tears begin streaming down my face.

"So," I continue, "All those months ago when we talked about those miners, I wasn't at the bottom of the well then, was I?"

She pauses, and looks at me, her expression full of sadness and regret.

"No, you weren't. But, we didn't know that then - neither of us did - and I'm not going to let you get to the bottom. You are too precious. Even if you can't see it, I can. You have too much to give, and too much to offer. I'm not going to let this take it all away from you."

Two days after that Zoom call, I find myself sitting on a bed in a Specialist Eating Disorder Unit, having just been detained under Section 3 of the Mental Health Act, feeling bewildered, alone and yet somehow, grateful. Grateful to have not *quite* reached the bottom of the well.

Chapter 2

The Drowning Metaphor

Life with anorexia is hard to put into words. To anyone looking in from the outside, it doesn't make a lot of sense, and that, I think, is understandable. Why would anyone want to starve themselves? To restrict their food to such an extent that they become a shell of a person, unable to take part in normal everyday activities, ending up in hospital, or in the most severe cases, dead. After all, starvation is a form of torture, once used in detention centres, concentration camps and prisons as a kind of extreme and unbearable punishment. In some places, it still is today.

When you put it like that, the whole thing sounds absurd. Why would anyone willingly put themselves through mental torture? What could they possibly have done to deserve such awful treatment? The answer, in most cases, is nothing. Absolutely nothing at all.

But for the sufferer, the person with anorexia, the illness itself is a bit of a paradox. As a rational, sentient being, you know that what you are doing is illogical, meaningless, a complete and utter waste of time. But you also know that when you're in it - and I mean *really* in it - it's the only thing in the world that makes sense. Every thought and every action feels absolutely necessary, as though your whole life depends on it.

If you were able to take a step back and engage the rational part of your brain for long enough, you might be able to see the situation differently, to recognise it for what it really is. But unfortunately, for someone caught in the cruel clutches of an eating disorder, stepping back and looking at the bigger picture feels about as doable as sprouting a pair of wings and flying off to live on the moon. The best way I can think of explaining it, is to say that it's a bit like drowning.

Imagine, for a moment, that you are swimming in the sea. You are using the same strokes and breathing techniques you've used many times before, and for a while, everything is fine. The sun is shining, and you might even go as far as to say that you're enjoying yourself. Until, all of a sudden, you notice that your muscles have started to ache, and you feel very, very tired.

"But that's normal, isn't it?" you say to yourself. "That's what swimming *should* feel like."

So you keep pushing, on and on, feeling yourself getting weaker and weaker, but still, you do not stop. Something in your head - a voice, not unlike your own - tells you to keep going. And that's exactly what you do. You keep swimming, even though it hurts (the pain is coursing through your body now, to the point that it's becoming hard to bear), and you desperately want to stop and rest. You keep swimming even though it's awful, because the voice in your head - the voice that you know and trust - is telling you that you are doing the right thing.

More time passes, and eventually, you reach what you think is your limit. You've had enough of swimming now. In fact, you hate it. You hate it and you want to stop. So, you reach down and try to put one foot on the bottom of the sea floor. You expect to feel soft sand brushing against your toes, but to your surprise, you don't feel anything at all. You try again. Still nothing. Treading water, you turn around to find that the shore is miles off, and you've swum a lot further than you realised. You are out of your depth.

In utter panic, you try to make your way back to the safety of the shallows, but you are so depleted, you simply don't have the strength. By now, you barely have the energy to hold your head above water, let alone break into a front crawl. So, you begin to drown. You gasp for air and move your arms in a futile attempt to keep yourself afloat, but it's no good. Instead of air, you inhale water, and you find yourself choking, gasping, choking, gasping, until eventually, your head falls below the surface. Now totally submerged, you feel an immense pressure, as though there's a hand on your head forcing you deeper and deeper below the surface. You want nothing more than to come up for air, and to be safely back on dry land, but it's no use. You know that if you stay under the water, you will drown, but there's nothing you can do. You are powerless. Totally, and utterly powerless.

That, in a nutshell, is what it feels like to live with anorexia.

Chapter 3
Tahini

"Sophia! Guess what?!"

Natalie, my best friend on the ward, bounds up to me, her short blond bob partially covered by a black woollen beanie, and a wild, indignant look in her blue-green eyes, the corners of each outlined with a delicate flick of kohl black liner.

"What?" I ask, my lips curling into a half smile, as though I already know she's going to tell me some sort of joke.

"I just tried tahini for the first time *ever...*" she exclaims.

"And?" I ask again, bracing myself for the punchline.

"And it tastes like absolute shit. I'm so livid. I just spent 6 quid on a massive jar of it."

I laugh, reaching out a hand to examine the jar before opening it and taking a sniff. The expression on my face reflects her sentiments exactly, and she looks triumphantly from me to the jar and back again, as though my grimace has proved her point.

"See? It's fucking rank isn't it? I just had it on a sweet potato and it was one of the most disgusting things I've ever put in my mouth. Do you want to try some?" she asks, waving a tablespoon in my direction.

"Yes *please*," I say with mock enthusiasm. "In fact, forget the spoon. You've given it such a glowing review I'll just eat the whole jar. With my hands."

She flops down next to me on the sofa, leans her head on my shoulder and says,

"Honestly Sophia, I don't get it. Everyone on Instagram is raving about it like it's some kind of nectar of the Gods, but it tastes like shit."

"Yeah, but what did we say about Instagram?" I ask her with a knowing grin.

"That it's all a fucking conspiracy. *I know.* It's probably half the reason I've ended up here. Instagram, and that stupid raw vegan diet. It's all bollocks, but it's *so* dangerous. I'm starting to think *everything* is a conspiracy. Even bloody Covid."

"Alright David Ike!" I say, giving her a wry smile. "Tahini isn't dangerous though. It's just disgusting," I point out matter of factly, still laughing at her, and realising as I do that this is the first time I've properly done so in months.

"Too right," she nods in agreement. "Imagine if they gave us all tahini as a meal replacement instead of Fortisip. We'd all be licking our plates clean!"

"Totally," I say, my eyes brimming with tears of laughter. "Although if the Consultant said she'd discharge me if I ate a whole jar of tahini, I think I'd do it. Actually, I'd probably eat a truckload of the stuff just to get out of here."

Natalie looks at me, beaming, and raises her jar of tahini as if making a toast. I pick up my tea, clink it against the glass jar, and say,

"Here's to another day in paradise. And to never eating tahini again as long as we live."

Chapter 4

Do You Want to Be a Supermodel?

I'm sitting outside the MDT room waiting to see the Consultant. There are two Consultants on the ward - Dr D and Dr Q - and I'm not technically Dr D's patient, but this is a bit of an emergency. You see, the thing is, I can't move. Over the past few days, I've become so anxious and on edge that every single muscle in my body has tensed up, and it's an immense effort even to go from sitting to a standing position.

Although highly unpleasant, unfortunately this feeling isn't new. It's something I experience on an almost daily basis, but until now, I've just accepted and tried to live with it. It wasn't until I first came to an eating disorder unit, and had to live with lots of other people, that I realised it wasn't normal to feel this way.

As I wait for Dr D to turn up, I do my best to prepare for the ordeal of having to stand and walk with him into the MDT room, where Ward Round, and the weekly 1:1s usually take place. All I really need is for him to increase my medication so that my muscles will start to relax and - hopefully - I'll be able to move around with a little more grace and poise than I currently am. Right now, I feel less like a young woman and more like an ancient rusty robot that badly needs oiling.

The Consultant arrives, and with his help, I manage to get into the room and sit down on a chair, although not without great difficulty. When he asks me what he can do to help, I do my best to put what I'm experiencing into words.

"I'm so on edge all the time. It's like every single muscle in my body has tensed up, and basically, I can't really move," I blurt out, my face beginning to redden with embarrassment, clashing violently with the bright orange jumper dress I am wearing.

"And when you add in the anorexia," I continue, "It's like being trapped in your body and your mind at the same time. It's horrible."

"I can imagine it must be," he says gently, looking me straight in the eye, his expression serious, and yet still warm and compassionate. Before I know it, I am crying, my whole body wracked with sobs.

"Well, we can't leave you like this," he says. "I'll certainly increase your medication. And once your muscles begin to relax, I think you'll start to feel better."

"Thank you," I say gratefully, wiping the tears from my eyes with the back of my hand.

He pauses for a moment, before asking me a very difficult question.

"How do you feel about your body?"

For some reason, this makes my cry even harder, and he waits patiently for me to compose myself before I try to come up with a coherent answer.

"I suppose…I resent it," I tell him tentatively. "I feel frustrated a lot of the time anyway, but it gets so much worse when things like this happen. I'm just angry at my body for letting me down, and I feel so, so trapped."

Dr D nods, making it clear that he understands where I'm coming from, before going straight in with another, equally difficult, question.

"And what about when you look in the mirror? How do you feel about what you see?"

"Erm…I hate it," I say matter-of-factly. "This probably sounds trivial and shallow, but I don't mean it in that way. It's not so much about what I look like as it is about how I feel."

"And how is that? How *do* you feel?" he asks.

"Disgusting. Just so, *so* disgusting that it's almost unbearable. Have you seen Big Hero 6?" I ask, knowing, as I do so, that this is a very weird question to be asking a Consultant.

He fixes his gaze on me for a moment, a quizzical and slightly amused look in his eyes.

"I haven't. What is it?" he asks, sounding genuinely intrigued.

"It's a Disney film. Or maybe Pixar, I can't remember. But anyway, there's a character in it who looks like a giant white blobby marshmallow. I feel like that," I tell him bluntly, without the slightest hint of emotion or humour in my voice.

I take out my phone and Google it to show him exactly what I mean, as though proving my point.

"I see," he says. His face is partially hidden by a mask, but I can tell that he's smiling, although not at all unkindly, and there's an empathic look in his large brown eyes.

"And is there anything that changes the way you feel about your body, and the way you look?" he asks.

"Well, restriction, obviously," I say. "It just makes me feel better. It takes some of the distress away, at least for a little while.

"But in here you can't do that, and you're struggling?" he asks, but we both know it's not really a question.

"Yes. Yes I am," I reply.

He takes another long pause, smiles from beneath his mask, then looks deep into my eyes and asks the most difficult question of all.

"And, can I ask, how do you feel about your disability, about your cerebral palsy? How do you feel about your body in relation to that?"

I think for a moment, wondering how honest I should be, but in the end I decide I've got nothing to lose.

"I do find it very hard. I always have, and I think part of me always will. It was difficult growing up feeling as though there was something wrong with me, and that I needed to be fixed. And when you're a child, you don't really know any different. You just sort of take things at face value. But I'm also a lot more accepting of it than I used to be. The older I get, the more I've come to realise that it's not *me* that's the problem. A lot of the time it's the environment I'm in, or other people's opinions of how a person - and a body - should be."

Dr D is quiet for a while, but I can tell he's smiling again, this time even more than before.

"That is such a good attitude. It's really, really positive," he says, a slight twinkle in his eye.

"Let me ask you something. What if someone told you that you aren't disgusting, and that you're actually a very beautiful young woman. What would you say to that?" he says.

I'm so taken aback, I don't know what to do or say, so I just stare at the floor, silently willing the ground to swallow me whole.

"I'm serious," he says. "You are a very beautiful young lady. You could be a model. You have the face and the figure, and with your story, I think it would inspire a lot of people. Do you want to be a supermodel? I mean, is it something you'd consider? My daughter works for a modelling agency. Would you like me to sort it out for you?"

By this point, I'm absolutely lost for words, so I keep quiet, hoping he'll change the subject back to my medication. When he doesn't I try to steer the topic back to where I need it to go.

"Honestly Dr D, all I want right now is to be able to move out of this chair. I only really came to see you for some diazepam."

"Okay, that's fair enough," he says, laughing, that familiar twinkle back in his eye. "But truthfully, I think you have what it takes. Keep it in mind for the future, and maybe we can talk about it again."

I thank him, tell him I'll think about it, and let him help me back out into the corridor, my cheeks as red as two ripe tomatoes.

Chapter 5
Paul and Dave

At the moment, there are two men in my life - Paul and Dave - who are proving to be a very bad influence. I don't recall the exact day or time that they came into my world, but ever since they made an appearance, they've both insisted on leading me - no, forcing me - down the wrong path, to a place that is very, very far away from where I want to be. Sort of like when you fall in with the wrong crowd at school, even though you know they're not good for you, and yet something about them keeps pulling you back. That's how it is for me, with Paul and Dave. I know they're always there, like two little devils perched on my shoulder, and I *know* they're not good for me, but no matter how hard I try, I just can't seem to shake them off. It really is like being in an abusive relationship.

Actually, that's not strictly true. Some days I do manage to get rid of them, briefly, but it's never long before I find myself being lured back into their clutches. I'm conscious that to an outsider, this probably isn't making a lot of sense, so I'll do my best to explain - firstly, who they really are, and secondly, how they got here.

I would say they're as bad as each other, but Paul is, without a doubt, the worst. Like I say, I can't quite remember exactly when he first appeared; perhaps he's been around for years without me ever really noticing, lurking under the surface and waiting for the right moment to pounce. But recently, in fact, for months on end, he's been leading me astray, and has made it his life mission to cause me as much harm as possible.

Being in hospital, you'd think I'd be safe, but every single day, he still manages to find a way to get me into trouble. And more than that, to hurt me. In the morning, I wake up with huge bruises on my forehead, and whenever I look in the mirror, all I can hear is Paul's voice, telling me that I'm not good enough, that I'm horrible, disgusting, repulsive even. That I need to tear the skin off my body, limb from limb, set myself on fire, bang my head against the wall repeatedly until the room is spinning and there are black dots in front of my eyes; essentially do whatever it takes to cause myself so much harm that I'm unable to think about anything else.

Of course, all of this sounds horrible, and in truth, it absolutely is. Whenever anyone asks me why I deserve to put myself through all this pain - indeed, through any pain at all - when I'm already going through so much, I don't have an answer. All I find myself able to say is "because I have to. Because it feels like the right thing to do. Because it feels like the *only* thing to do."

But this is just it. It never feels like a choice, mostly because Paul is very sneaky. Every time he makes an appearance, chiming in with yet another suggestion, demanding that I start my day by doing this or that, instead of simply waking up, getting showered, dressed and having breakfast like a 'normal' person, I find it so hard to fight against it, and most of the time end up giving in and doing exactly what he wants. I've asked myself why on many occasions, and every time I come up with the same answer (spoiler alert: it's not a good one). Because he says it will help me. Because he says it will take the pain away. Because he says that, of all the options I have, this is the one that will make it all better.

I want to make it clear that deep down, I know none of this is true. I'm not naive. I know I'm not a bad person. I know I don't deserve pain. And I've lived on this earth long enough to know that replacing one pain with another isn't the solution to any of my problems. But in the dark moments - of which, lately, there are many - Paul is so convincing that I really *do* feel I have no option but to give in to his awful demands, all under the pretence that doing so will make everything okay.

When I think about it like this, and when I write it all down on paper, I almost can't believe I've ended up in this situation; that it really is *me* behaving like this and allowing myself to do these things, when all I'm actually doing is prolonging my own suffering. But right now, this is just how it is. I'm fighting against it, of course I am. And I'll continue to fight until Paul is gone and all of this is nothing but a distant, albeit painful, memory.

Now I've told you about Paul, it's only right that I talk about Dave. As I said at the start, they're both very, *very* different, but I can't deny that neither of them are a good influence on me. They both drag me down and, ultimately, stop me from getting where I need to go, only in completely different ways. While Paul is pretty much pure evil - a real, out and out bad guy - Dave is a bit more subtle. Really and truly, it was never my choice to have him in my life. He was forced upon me, a bit like an old unwanted heirloom from a very distant Great Aunt. I don't want him there, but as things stand, I need him, and that is something I can hardly even bring myself to admit. I said I can't recall how he got here, but that's not quite right. Truthfully, I remember the day like it was yesterday, and I know it'll probably stay imprinted in my memory for a very long time.

It was the 25th of December 2021, and after having breakfast and opening a few presents, I received the worst gift of all. I got given Dave. And ever since then, he's been weighing down on me like a millstone around my neck, a constant reminder of my eating disorder, and of just how powerful it's become. Looking back on that day, I remember feeling deflated and defeated, but also an odd sense of relief - one which, even now, I struggle to put into words. Although I hate to admit it, I think perhaps this relief came from knowing that - at least for a while - I didn't have to worry about eating anything other than breakfast. As long as I had Dave by my side, I could have my Weetabix - one of my only 'safe foods' - in relative peace, knowing that I didn't have to wage war against anorexia again until the next day. Of course, I still had to gain weight, but even so, I didn't really have to think too much about it. With Dave around, pumping away behind the scenes, I could try to convince myself that none of this was really happening, and get on with the day as best I could.

Anyone reading this will know as well as I do that it was just classic avoidance, which in any area of life, is absolutely no good, but especially when you have an eating disorder. But as I say, for a short while each day, having Dave allowed me a little peace of mind, and that is something which, at the time, I was very *very* grateful for.

In case you haven't guessed, Dave is not a person, but the name I have unaffectionately given my feed bag. Connected through a tube that goes into my nose, down my throat and straight into my stomach, he provides me with the nutrition I need everyday, but that, because of my eating disorder, I am unable to manage myself.

As the days and weeks have passed, gradually I've come to rely on Dave less and less, and although the anorexia is still very *very* strong, I know in my heart that one day soon, I'll be free of him - and Paul - forever. And when that day finally comes, I'll never, ever want to look back.

Chapter 6

Diazepam and Tom and Jerry

One Friday lunchtime, I am in the downstairs dining room fetching the ice cream that is needed every day for dessert. We have a freezer upstairs on the ward, so why they don't just store it in there is beyond me, but if I complained about all the idiosyncrasies in this hospital, this book would be about as long as *War and Peace*.

The dining room is bustling, the air is ringing with general chatter and the sound of knives and forks clatters on plates. Already anxious, the ordinariness of it sets my teeth on edge and all I can think about is getting back upstairs, away from all the noise - and, of course - the food. Scanning around the room for something to focus on, I catch sight of one of the Consultants out of the corner of my eye. He's a tall black man in his late sixties, and without the obligatory standard issue blue face mask, I'm able to see his whole face properly for the first time, and can't help but notice how kind and gentle he looks; like the grandfather everyone wishes they had. Not least because he dolls out diazepam (which he refers to as 'the miracle drug') as though it's going out of fashion, and his favourite phrases are *"stay cool"* and *"live long and prosper."* As always, he's the embodiment of calm, so relaxed and at ease that he's almost horizontal. Whenever I look at him, I can't help but envy him and wonder how he does it.

On the table in front of him is an empty plate smeared with the remnants of today's dessert - chocolate fudge cake and vanilla ice cream - and a bowl of tomato soup which he's just begun eating. In that moment, a quote by the French pastry chef Jacques Torres springs to mind: 'Life is short. Eat dessert first," and in spite of my jangling nerves, I can't help but smile. From where I'm standing, I notice that he's watching something on his mobile phone, but through the cluster of tables and chairs, I can't quite see what it is, so I edge slowly towards him to take a closer look, all the while trying not to disturb his slightly unorthodox lunch. Since he's a Consultant, and by all accounts, a very clever man, I half expect to find him watching the news, or the recording of some kind of psychiatry conference, but to my surprise - and delight - I see that he's engrossed in an episode of Tom and Jerry, giggling away to himself as the two characters career around on the screen. I laugh without meaning to, and he turns around to look at me, a wide grin on his face and a twinkle in his eye. Ever since I got here, I've wondered what his secret is; how he manages to stay so impossibly - annoyingly - relaxed, and now, it seems, I've found out: chocolate cake - eaten before the main course - diazepam, and a daily dose of Tom and Jerry.

Chapter 7

All I Eat is Weetabix

It's 8.30 in the morning and I'm sitting down to a bowl of luke-warm brown mush that is both the colour and texture of wallpaper paste. Currently, other than the occasional yoghurt or cup of Fortisip, this is the only thing that ever passes my lips. It's also one of the only times I ever set foot in the dining room, but if you'd ever been in there yourself, I'm pretty sure you wouldn't blame me. In case you've never witnessed it, I'll give you a bit of an insight, although, of course, I can only speak from my own experience.

Really and truly, the dining room in an EDU is just like any other dining room anywhere in the world.

That is, if everyone present has just found out their closest friend has died, *and* been told that the food they're about to eat is laced with a deadly poison. The radio is always on full blast, and the sound of cutlery clattering on plates is just as jarring as fingernails scraping along a blackboard. If you gave me the option of going into the dining room or walking across a layer of hot coals, the chances are I'd much rather do the latter. That's how unpleasant it really is.

Don't get me wrong, all of the other patients are absolutely lovely. And, outside of a dining room context I get along with most of them very well, but throw any food into the equation and it's a totally different story. But of course, if the situation were any different, we probably wouldn't need to be here.

Later that afternoon, I'm in the kitchen with a few other patients and a member of staff. Everyone else has had their snack and sat through supervision, and are making cups of tea and coffee to take with them to their rooms or into the garden, since the sun has decided to make an appearance for once. I am not having snack, since Dave is whirring away on my back taking care of that, but I am having a cup of biscuit-flavoured tea, which, at this point in time, is pretty much the only thing I ever drink. The member of staff sitting with me is also having a hot drink, and as she goes over to the cupboard to choose a packet of biscuits, she turns around and asks me if I've had snack, or if I'd like some biscuits.

If you have an eating disorder, or have ever been to an inpatient EDU, you'll already know that this isn't really the most appropriate thing to say to a patient (especially one on an NG feed), but I know she didn't mean any harm, so although there are probably times when I would have taken offence, in that moment, I don't mind at all. So, instead of getting upset, or storming off in a huff, I respond with this:

"First of all, you *know* I don't have snack. I'm quite literally carrying it on my back," I tell her, pointing matter-of-factly to Dave. "And secondly, even if I wasn't, I wouldn't touch a biscuit if you gave me a thousand pounds."

"Why not?" She asks, innocently, as though she's had a momentary memory lapse and forgotten where she is.

"Not even one? Or *half* of one. That's nothing!" she pleads, as though bargaining with me.

"No. Not even half of one," I tell her defiantly.

"But *why?*" she pleads again, laughing with me now, even though I know she's deadly serious, and that if she saw me eat even a few crumbs of a digestive, she'd probably cry with happiness.

"Because that's just not my vibe right now," I tell her with a grin, even though, really, nothing about this conversation is funny. "And, as everyone here knows, all I eat is Weetabix. I've got Dave here to deal with everything else."

"Who is Dave?" she asks, looking confused.

"My feed bag," I say matter-of-factly. "I spend enough time carrying it around on my back so I figured I might as well give it a name," I tell her with a grin.

"Oh, I see," she says with a look of disappointment. "Well, you know what I think, Soph? One day soon, I know you'll do it. You'll get rid of Dave and you'll surprise everyone - even yourself. No one can live off Weetabix forever."

Chapter 8

Hummus Is Not For Us

"Many people will walk in and out of your life, but only true friends will leave footprints in your heart"
– Eleanor Roosevelt

A few days have passed since the tahini episode, and some of us are in the lounge talking about hummus. After covering the usual topics such as taste, texture, what it goes well with and what it doesn't, and how, because Natalie eats so much of it, it might as well be coursing through her veins, we somehow move on to discussing its origins (yes, we really are *that* bored. Outside of meals, snacks and supervision, there is very little to do in an EDU).

Since all we have to go on is guesswork and speculation, we're probably spouting utter nonsense, but as none of us are hummus experts, it matters very little that we have no idea what we're talking about. The main topic of our debate is how hummus can be so nice when it essentially consists of mushed up chickpeas and tahini - aka the food of the devil.

"I just don't get it," Natalie exclaims, looking incredulously from me to the other patients and back again.

"How can hummus be so delicious when it's basically just tahini, chickpeas, a bit of oil, and lemon juice?"

"I dunno," I say laughing, "There's got to be some kind of sorcery going on somewhere. They must have some real skills to disguise the taste of that stuff. It's *so* bitter!"

"Who's they?" Leila pipes up from across the room. A half British, half Iranian girl who had to drop out of medical school because of her anorexia, she's been on the ward for over a year and yet she still won't let so much as a teaspoonful of hummus - or anything else for that matter - come within five feet of her.

"Well, Middle Eastern people I guess. Hummus is Middle Eastern isn't it?" I ask, my words more of a question than a statement, since, much like Leila, I haven't so much as sniffed a pot of hummus in over a year.

"I don't know. I could be wrong, but I *think* it's probably Iranian," she says matter-of-factly.

"What?!" A voice chimes in almost accusingly, as though we'd been plotting to set the hospital on fire, not discussing the origins of a popular chickpea-based dip.

The person speaking is Pardis, one of the HCAs. Born and raised in Iran, she came to England to study Psychology at university and has stayed here ever since. She's intelligent, caring, and beautiful, with a face and figure that resembles Disney's Princess Jasmine, but in spite of all of this, her confidence leaves something to be desired. With two Master's degrees under her belt, her English is unsurprisingly very good, but she doubts herself a lot, and can usually be found scribbling words and phrases on the palm of her hand which she later transcribes into a notebook, all in an effort to improve her vocabulary.

Just as she goes out of her way to learn new things, she's also one of those people who goes above and beyond for us without a second thought, always taking time out of her day to run errands, support people, or offer an empathetic listening ear. She is, without a doubt, my favourite member of staff on the ward, and more than that, one of the loveliest people I've ever met. So much so, that I wish we could be friends in real life.

"Yeah, Pardis, hummus is Iranian isn't it? Or if not, it's definitely from somewhere in the Middle East," I ask, hoping I haven't revealed the fact that my knowledge of geography is at best, patchy, and at worst, totally abismal.

"No!" She exclaims, evidently quite offended by what I've just said. From the look on her face I can't tell whether she's joking, but I hope she is, since bad-mouthing her country and upsetting her is the last thing I'd want to do.

"Hummus is not for us!" She shouts, now clearly in mock outrage.

"Hummus is not for us?" Leila asks, parroting the phrase back at her in exactly the same high-pitched tone and laughing as she does it. "What does that mean?"

"No! Hummus is not for us!" Pardis says again, offering no explanation whatsoever.

"Pardis, what are you talking about? You're not making any sense," I say, tears of laughter starting to well up in my eyes.

"I *mean* hummus is not for us. Hummus is not Iranian, it's Lebanese. You can't blame *this* on Iran!" she exclaims, smiling widely as she does so and indicating to me that she isn't really offended.

"Oh Pardis, you're *hilarious!*" Leila says emphatically. "Hummus is not for us. What an amazing expression. Tonight, when they bring our jacket potatoes and hummus up from the kitchen for dinner, that's what we should all say to get out of eating it. *'Hummus is not for us!'* In fact, I think we should all get it printed onto t-shirts and wear them around the ward. It could be like a new hospital uniform, only for patients instead of staff."

"This is brilliant," I agree. "The next time the Consultant tries to talk about my meal plan in Ward Round, I'm just gonna pull the 'hummus is not for us' card and see how she reacts. I bet she'll think I'm even more nuts than she already does. It's lucky you can't section someone twice, otherwise she'd probably end up doing it again and I'd be stuck in here for years. Still, I reckon it'd be worth it though. *"Hummus is not for us!"* I shout, turning to Pardis and beaming from ear to ear.

9

Mirtazapine And Custard Creams

"Sophia! Something terrible has happened!"

Natalie bursts into my room, looking stricken.

"What is it?" I ask in alarm, her sense of urgency making me wonder whether she's about to announce the start of World War III.

"I just spilled organic green tea on my £60 yoga mat," she wails, sitting down next to me on my bed, her beige high-waisted chinos rolled up just below her knees.

"Oh," I say, feeling very underwhelmed by her news, but trying to pretend I'm treating the situation with the seriousness she feels it demands.

"And that's not all!" she wails again, her face screwed up in agony.

"No? You mean there's something else?" I ask, trying desperately to stifle a laugh.

"No!" She moans, looking me straight in the eye. "The carbs have moved to my ankles!"

"The carbs have done what?" I ask. "What are you talking about? That's not even a thing," I tell her matter-of-factly, now unable to stop myself from laughing at the horrified expression on her face.

"Look! Just look at my legs! They're like fucking balloons. I feel like Mr Blobby or something. What the hell is going on? It must be the Mirtazapam," she says incredulously.

A few days ago, one of the Consultants, Dr Q, started Natalie on a Mirtazapine, an antidepressant that's supposed to help with low mood and sleep, because of its slightly sedative effect.

"You mean Mirtazapine?" I say, laughing. "Surely she hasn't put you on a cocktail of Mirtazapine and Diazepam - that'd be lethal. You wouldn't be able to keep your eyes open!"

"Yeah, that's what I mean. What's it called? Mirtazapine. It's made me feel a bit calmer, which I love, but I've swelled up like a bloody inflatable. I don't know what to do," she says helplessly. I can hear the panic rising in her voice. "I feel like a bouncy castle."

"Erm…you could always stop taking it I guess. But how do you know it's definitely that? It could just be water retention or something."

"It *must* be. It's only been happening since Dr Q started me on the Mirtazapam, and at first I didn't really care, but now it's driving me insane. I can't keep going like this - I'll explode!"

"Have you spoken to her about it?" I ask.

"Yeah. Twice. *And* I showed her my legs," she says triumphantly, as though proving a point.

"Right. So what did she say?" I ask, with genuine intrigue.

"Nothing much. Just that this is what happens to some people, and that she'd keep an eye on it. But it's fucking insane. Also I can't stop thinking about custard creams," she says, her eyes wild with a mixture of excitement and what I *think* must be fear.

"Custard creams?" I ask. "What about them?"

"I just want to eat them *all the fucking time.* Honestly, they're all I can think about. Before I came here, I hadn't so much as touched one for years, and now I'm obsessed with them. What the fuck is going on?"

"Well, why don't you have some?" I say tentatively, feeling as though I'm stating the obvious. Natalie is on the ward's Transition programme, which basically means that she can eat whatever she wants, whenever she wants, without anyone so much as batting an eyelid.

"That's the thing. I *have.* I've just smashed two whole packets. I swear I ate them all in about 30 seconds," she tells me, sounding both proud and a little bit horrified.

"Oh. But when you say 'packets' you mean those little packs of three they have in the kitchen, right? Not like massive multipacks from Asda?" I ask, trying unsuccessfully to stifle a laugh.

"Yeah, yeah. Only the small packets. But still. I've never been so obsessed with food like this in my life. It's driving me mad."

"Well, you can absolutely tell me I'm wrong here, but does it really matter? Even if you *had* eaten 50 custard creams it wouldn't be the end of the world. Your body is obviously craving it. Maybe you should listen to it and give it what it wants?"

I'm careful to pose that last statement as a question so that Natalie doesn't call me out for being a massive hypocrite, since, right now, the only thing I eat is Weetabix.

"Yeah, I guess so. But I had a massive binge last night as well. I had a main dessert and *then* I demolished a whole tub of Booja Booja ice cream."

For anyone that doesn't already know, Booja Booja is a brand of fancy vegan confectionery, and yes, it really is as boujee and expensive as it sounds. Last time I checked, it was about £6 a tub, so really, I think it should be rebranded as 'Boujee Boujee ice cream.

"Okay." I say, speaking very slowly and deliberately because I want her to know I'm taking the situation seriously, rather than simply laughing at her misfortune.

"But did you enjoy it? The ice cream I mean. Even if you think it was a binge."

"Yeah, it's bloody incredible. I just wish I hadn't eaten so much of it. I'm going to put on so much weight," she says, the wild look back in her eyes.

Again, I'm conscious of stating the obvious or offending her, so I say gently,

"Isn't that half the point of being here though?" I say, laughing at her in spite of myself. "To put on weight?"

"Well yeah. But not *this* much, and not in all the wrong places. I mean, I *love* having boobs and a bum. I've never had boobs like this in my life. I keep looking down at them and being like, 'Oooh hello!' But the rest of it is sending me crazy. *How do I make it stop?!*"

She looks at me, half pleading, half laughing, and we fall back onto the bed, overcome by a fit of giggles that borders on delirium.

"I really don't know," I say, in between laughs, "but I want you to remember that I'll still love you no matter what. Even if you do look like Mr Blobby."

Chapter 10
Let's Get It On

Following the discussion in my most recent Ward Round, the Consultant has decided that allowing me to have a bath without someone watching me - in fact, allowing me to do *anything* without someone watching me - presents too much of a risk given my current mental state, so if I want to have a bath or shower, or even just go to the toilet, I'll have no choice but to do it in full view of a member of staff. So, tonight, I had my first supervised bath, and it was without a doubt one of the strangest experiences of my life.

I took some toiletries, a towel, and a pair of pyjamas from my room before heading downstairs to the bathroom on the ground floor - the only place in the hospital with a bath. Once inside, I started to run the water, putting in some bubble bath and a bath bomb in an attempt to make the whole experience a little bit nicer and more 'normal', and waited what felt like an age for the tub to fill up to an acceptable level. Although, of course, not so much that anyone might think I was going to try and drown myself.

Once it was done, I turned off the hot water tap - which, at best could only ever be described as luke-warm - and tried to work out how I could get undressed in a way that would preserve even the tiniest shred of my dignity. I thought about closing the shower curtain and trying to somehow hide behind it, but before I'd so much as reached up to grab a hold of it, the staff member shook her head as if to say "not a chance in hell." It was almost as though she had read my mind.

"Uh uh," she said, shaking her head again and wagging one of her long painted fingernails at me. "I need to be able to see *eve-ry-thing*, and you know that only too well. But don't worry, you ain't got nothing under there that I haven't seen before," she told me stoically, gesturing from my head, to my baggy jumper, all the way down to my long skirt and Doc Martens. "I see you tryna cover up, but just get those spindle legs out and get in that bath before the water goes colder than it already is." She flashes me a wicked, knowing smile, clearly both pleased and unsurprised that she'd been able to read my thoughts quite so accurately.

Reluctantly, I do as I'm told, trying not to think about the idea that I'm about to reveal my naked body to a relative stranger, and focusing instead on the fact that the bath bomb has turned the water a vibrant shade of pink. Stretching my powers of imagination as far as they'll go, I do my best to pretend I'm in a spa or a branch of Lush instead of a freezing cold, fluorescently lit bathroom in a psych ward with no toilet seat, no taps, and no lock on the door.

I peel my clothes off one by one, hoping that if I do everything at a snail's pace, I'll have time to mentally prepare myself for what's about to happen. As I do so, I feel every inch of myself tensing up, and I can't help but wince at the idea that there's someone standing behind me watching me undress, staring at my body when I can't even bear to look at it myself.

Although rationally I know I can't be as big as I think I am, this new body, one that feels horribly, overwhelmingly huge, is just so foreign, so alien, and so unlike the one I am used to, that it makes me want to tear my skin off. It's at times like that a quote by the author Miranda July comes to mind. I stumbled across it years ago, but to this day it is still one of the most relatable sentences I've ever read: *"All I ever really want to know is how other people are making it through life - where do they put their body, hour by hour, and how do they cope inside of it?"*

Once all my clothes are off, I step into the bath, placing one hand on the side of the sink and the other on the wall to steady myself, before lowering myself into the brightly coloured, luke-warm water. Staring down at it now, the colour seems to have transformed from a pretty bubble-gum pink into something much more garish, clashing horribly with the clinical fluorescent lighting, and I feel less like I'm in a spa and more like Winona Ryder in *Girl Interrupted*, except I'm not even allowed to use a razor.

As I sit in the lurid pink water, having strategically positioned the bubbles in an attempt to preserve even the tiniest ounce of modesty, I'm overcome by a sense of what - I think - must be shame. Shame at the fact that I'm sitting naked in front of a woman I don't know. Shame at the size of my body. Shame at the shape of it, the weight of it, the feel of it. Shame at the fact that my eating disorder has landed me in hospital yet again. Shame at the fact all of my friends are out in the world having babies and getting married and buying houses and going on holidays and moving up in their careers while I'm locked in here crying over yoghurt and jacket potatoes. Shame at the thought of everything and nothing, all at once.

Although I'm not crying, or showing any obvious signs of distress, the member of staff with me senses something isn't right, and does her best to lighten the mood.

"It's boring in here," she says brightly. "Let's put some music on. What do you like?"

Before I even have a chance to open my mouth, she takes out her phone, opens Spotify, puts on 'La Bamba' by Los Lobos and starts dancing around the tiny bathroom, swinging her hips and clapping along to the beat. When it gets to the chorus, she starts spinning around, singing "Bam-ba bam-ba, bam-ba, bam-ba, bam-ba bam-ba, para bailar la bamba ay y arriba y arriba" at the top of her voice as though she's having the time of her life. As the song finishes, she lets out a long breath, bends over with her hands on her knees, looks at me and says, "why didn't you join in? I don't know how *anyone* can listen to that song without dancing. It's got me in the party mood and I've got another 10 hours of work to go but all I wanna do is shake my booty."

"Well, it *is* a good song," I admit, "but first of all I'm in the bath, so I'm a bit tight on space, and secondly, in case you haven't noticed, I'm butt naked," I say, laughing.

"So what?" she says, her face breaking into another wide grin. You can still dance! You can *always* dance. Anyway, let's switch things up a bit."

She sits down on a metal waste paper bin in the corner of the room and starts scrolling through her phone, looking for another song to play. Feeling more awkward than I probably ever have in my life, I sit in the tepid water, unable to predict what might be coming next, when all of a sudden the lights turn off and the whole room is plunged into darkness.

"Ah, these bloody things are on a sensor. They switch themselves off if you stop moving even for 10 seconds! Whoever invented them must have a screw loose," she says, still staring down at her phone, which is now the only source of light.

After a few seconds, the opening chords of Marvin Gaye's 'Let's get it on' start to play, and as I sit there in the pitch black, completely naked, I can't help but wonder where it all went so wrong. In spite of all the negatives and uncertainties surrounding me, in that moment I know one thing for sure: that this bath will go down in history as one of the most surreal experiences I've ever had.

11

I Feel Like a Persian Rug

"Your body is more than a thing to be looked at. It works with you, not against you. You do not beat your own heart." – Florence Welch

Ok, so here's the thing. Today, I'm wearing trousers. If you don't have an eating disorder, this might not sound like a big deal, but for me, it is huge. I haven't so much as looked at a pair of trousers for almost a year, and yet this morning, I threw caution to the wind and actually put some on. It's been a long time coming, and although I wish I could say it was a spur of the moment decision, I had to plan the whole thing with military precision. I scrolled through the Zara app trying to find some that I could actually tolerate, and after hours of searching, finally stumbled across what looked like the perfect pair. Soft and stretchy, with bold floral patterns, they were the clothing equivalent of a cross between William Morris wallpaper, and a Persian rug. Naturally, I thought they suited me down to a tee, so I bit the bullet and placed the order.

When they arrived, I took them out of the packaging with the utmost care, as though they were some sort of precious artefact that needed to be handled with kid gloves. As I did so, I was overcome by a heady combination of anticipation and fear. "What if they don't fit me?" I thought, panic starting to bubble up inside the pit of my stomach like honeycomb. "*What if they're too small?*"

Again, if you don't have an eating disorder, this probably doesn't seem like much of an issue. If you have a 'normal' (and by that I mean a non-anorexia-riddled) brain, I imagine you'd just feel a little annoyed at having to go through the rigmarole of sending them back, before simply buying the next size up. But to me, it felt as though my entire sense of self worth was dependent on whether or not these trousers fit.

Knowing I'd gone up several clothes sizes in the last few months - which is sort of a given, since the whole point of being in an EDU is to, y'know, put on weight - I looked at the measurements on the size guide and tried to work out which one I might be. This in itself felt like a mammoth task, because when you have body dysmorphia, it's almost impossible to accurately calculate your size and shape. Of course, as with most things, there are good days and bad days, but on the whole, it's not unusual for me to look in the mirror and conclude that I'm the size of three double decker buses. So, as you might imagine, there was quite a lot of to-ing and fro-ing before I finally decided what to put in my basket.

When I use the words 'body dysmorphia', I'm conscious that there might be some misconceptions flying around, or assumptions that this relates only to how someone looks in the sense of physical attractiveness, having a socially acceptable body size and shape, or 'being thin'. Although obviously I can only speak for myself, body dysmorphia - and body image - are about so, so much more than what I look like or what I see in the mirror.

While it does affect how I see myself, it is not, and has never been, a purely aesthetic thing. For me personally, body dysmorphia is more of a feeling, or even an emotion. At times, the sensations I experience are so intense, so all-consuming, and so horribly overwhelming that I won't be able to leave the house, or even speak to anyone on the phone. Like many intense feelings, it tends to come in waves; some of which I'm able to surf, while others drive me into the ground with the force and weight of a tsunami, leaving me with absolutely no option but to throw myself at their mercy, ending up totally submerged and on the brink of drowning.

As hard as I might be trying, it's very difficult to put any of this into words, but if I had to pick just one to describe this sensation, it would probably be 'disgust'. Although somehow, even that isn't quite right. It seems too trite and too simple to convey something so palpable, tangible and visceral as what I experience every day. But maybe I'm over-complicating things (it certainly wouldn't be the first time). Maybe Jack Kerouac was right when he said, "One day I will find the right words, and they will be simple."

Anyway, to cut a long(ish) story short, I bought some trousers from Zara and today, I put them on for the very first time. As soon as I left my room, I immediately wanted to run back inside and cocoon myself in the familiar safety of a baggy jumper and a long flowing dress or skirt, but for some reason, I didn't. I kept the trousers on, and for the rest of the day, I received more compliments than I think I ever have in my life. I wish I could say I accepted them gracefully, but truthfully, whenever someone told me I looked nice, I just replied with, "Erm, thanks. I feel like a Persian rug."

Chapter 12

Tracy's Socks

There's a member of staff on the ward - let's call her Tracy - who is, without a doubt, one of the most fascinating women I've ever come across in my life. And in case you can't tell, that is not a compliment.

She's a HCA, but in all the time she's worked here, I've never once seen her assist, or engage in anything that could ever be described as health care. She just wanders around the ward the way someone might walk around a park; that is, if they're a bit lost, and they really, *really* don't want to be there. She never says so much as a 'hello' to any of the patients, and if someone ever has the audacity to ask her to do anything that might be classed as 'work', she'll make an excuse before miraculously disappearing, quicker than an anorexic at a buffet.

Not only does she know nothing about eating disorders, she also seems to have almost no interpersonal skills, and about as much emotional intelligence and compassion as a shoe. To make matters worse, she's studying general nursing, so although I class myself as a stout atheist, I'll spend the rest of my days praying to a God I don't believe in that I never have the misfortune to ever end up as one of her patients.

Having said all of this, it's not in my interests to slag her, or anyone, off. That's not what this book is about. Most of the staff on the unit - in fact nearly all of them - are absolutely incredible, and their continued support has made a very difficult journey that little bit easier. And to give credit where credit is due, even Tracy has done her bit; albeit accidentally. Because when someone is this bad at their job, especially in an EDU, you just can't help but laugh.

In fact, I'd go as far as to say that in spite of all her faults (of which there are many), Tracy has actually managed to improve my mental health quite significantly. And not just once, but on a number of occasions - the funniest of which involving her eclectic, unconventional, and downright ridiculous dress sense.

I think it's fair to say that socks and sandals have long been considered a crime against fashion (that is, if you ignore the recent lockdown 'socks and sliders' trend), but during her time on the unit, Tracy has somehow managed to take this to the next level.

One evening, she turned up wearing an ensemble that was not only against the hospital uniform policy, and highly inappropriate for a night shift on a psych ward, but also (and most importantly) fucking hilarious. It consisted of a garish printed kaftan, a pencil skirt, bright pink, knee-length socks, and a pair of brown gladiator sandals.

On the night in question, I was still reeling from what had been a particularly horrendous day, but seeing Tracy sporting an outfit almost as tragic as her nursing skills - not to mention her personality - cheered me up no end. That night, I laughed in a way I thought I was no longer capable of: until my stomach ached and tears were rolling down my cheeks. I know I shouldn't have, but I even sneaked a photo which I set as my screensaver, and now, every time I look at my phone, it never fails to make me smile. It just goes to show how sometimes, even the smallest, silliest thing can make a big difference.

Chapter 13

Fumiland

Like Tracy, Fumi - another HCA - is also one of the most fascinating people I've ever met in my life, but this time, it absolutely *is* a compliment. If Tracy walks around the hospital like a very bad-tempered person who's found themselves lost in a park, Fumi is the total opposite. She strolls around the ward as if she owns the place, or even better, as though she's a visitor and everyone should count themselves lucky that she's graced them with her presence. She's never, ever in a rush - that is, unless it's time for lunch - and if you can't find her, you can bet your life savings that she'll be in the kitchen eating custard creams with all the cream scraped out, or one of her world-famous breakfast concoctions.

I've seen her make this 'breakfast' on countless occasions, but every single time I witness it, I end up in a fit of giggles. So much so that it makes my day. She starts with a layer of bran flakes, before adding cornflakes, muesli, grapes, yoghurt, custard (yes, custard), fruit salad, nuts and raisins, all finished off with a big dollop of peanut butter. Then, she proceeds to mix it all up together so that it just looks like a bowl of custard-y, yoghurt-y mess, before tucking in with the enthusiasm of a five-year-old at a birthday party. She's offered me a spoonful a few times, to which I've always (unsurprisingly) politely declined, but I still can't help but wonder what it tastes like, and more importantly, what possessed her to put all of those ingredients into a bowl at once. In any case, she always seems to be enjoying it, so who am I to question her preferences?

It's not only her taste in food that's unconventional. Everything about Fumi is eccentric. She must be in her early 60s, but she has both the dress sense and sense of humour of a 21-year-old. Playing games with her - in fact, doing *anything* with her - is absolutely hilarious; it's almost as though she's on another planet. She seems to have no concept of time, once hollering "BREEEEEAAAAKKFAAAAST" when it was 5.45pm and pitch black outside and I often think it's a wonder she remembers any of our names. In fact, she doesn't; there are times when she just seems to make them up, to the point where she's totally re-christened one patient, insisting on calling her 'Loose-Linda' instead of Lucinda, no matter how many times someone tries to correct her.

I want to stress that this isn't a slur on her character - far from it. If anything, I wish more people were like Fumi because the world would be a better (and much more amusing) place. In fact, I wish *I* was more like Fumi. Whenever I'm having a bad day - which, on the ward, tends to happen very frequently - I try to imagine what it might be like to spend a day in her brain.

One morning, right at the start of my admission, Fumi was preparing breakfast for all of us. She checked the meal plans, measured out the right amount of milk, and poured the correct cereal into the bowls, each one accompanied by either juice, or a piece of fruit. When she reached the last bowl, she added some Weetabix, then picked up an orange, cut it in half, and proceeded to squeeze the juice all over the cereal as though it was the most normal thing in the world. When the poor patient sat down in front of her milk and already soggy Weetabix, she looked aghast.

"Fumi, what's happened to my cereal? It's all wet, and it smells of oranges," she asked, clearly on the verge of tears.

"What do you mean, my darling? Your meal plan says Weetabix and an orange, so that's what you've got. *What is the problem*?" she replied, smiling and swaying from foot to foot, clearly far more invested in Capital radio's morning playlist than the fact that she was supposed to be supervising breakfast.

The more I've got to know Fumi, the more I've begun to think of her mind as being a bit like an amusement park - one which I've affectionately named 'Fumiland.' Having discussed this idea with some of the other girls on the ward, we've since come up with a pretty fantastical idea of how it might look, and whenever we're feeling a bit blue or homesick, we close our eyes and imagine that we're spending a day in Fumiland, and suddenly everything seems a lot brighter.

To get in, you must knock on the door and wait for Fumi's booming, excitable voice to shout, 'COME IN IF YOU'RE GOOD LOOKING' in her sing-song Nigerian accent. Once inside, you'll be handed a bowl of her custard-yoghurt breakfast cocktail, before spending the rest of the day meandering around, riding on spinning tea-cups and ferris wheels to your heart's content, all while listening to an upbeat mix of funk, soul, motown and reggae. And when you're tired (because it takes a lot of energy to have this much fun), you'll sit down on a huge squashy sofa, put your feet up, and enjoy a nice cup of coffee and some biscuits while reading the *Daily Mail*, just like Fumi does whenever she's on her break.

Her smiling face is emblazoned on massive holographic billboards all around the place, and everything is decorated with a wonderfully garish combination of leopard print and rainbows. You'll never have to leave, because time restrictions don't exist, and if you get peckish, all you have to do is click your fingers, and a packet of croissants or a Greggs' steak bake will magically appear in your hands. You'll be happy all the time, because in Fumiland that's the only rule, and if anyone ever does anything to annoy you, you can just dance away in the opposite direction, shouting 'I'M NOT HERE', the way Fumi does whenever anyone tries to get her attention and she's not in the mood to be summoned. Basically, it's the best amusement park in the world.

Chapter 14

A Walk in The Park

It's a Monday afternoon and I've just had the most brutal Ward Round of my life. Unable to articulate myself or get even the slightest hint of my point across, I just screamed and shouted and cried before storming out of the room and heading straight in the direction of the nearest wall.

Before I have the chance to get there and begin taking all my anger and frustration out on myself (thanks to Paul), I feel a hand on my arm and hear a voice saying, "No, Sophia. This way."

I turn around to see Meg, one of the nurses, eyeing me with a look that is stern but also kind. A look that says "I want to help, and what I'm about to do is for your own good."

"I know where you're trying to go, but I'm not letting you do that - not while you're with me. Not today", she says in the same firm but gentle tone, as though letting me know that when it comes to any form of self harm, I haven't got a chance in hell.

Still overwhelmingly frustrated and not sure how to respond, I stare back at her, burst into tears and let her pull me into a hug.

"What happened? What's upsetting you? Is it Ward Round?" she asks, a look of warmth and concern on her face.

I nod silently, tears streaming down my cheeks, unable to do anything but cry.

"Come on", she says, taking me by the hand and leading me down the corridor, placing herself strategically between me and any walls we pass along the way.

"Where are we going?" I ask her, my voice choked with tears.

"We're going for a walk. You need to get some fresh air, it'll help. And while we're out, if you want to, you can tell me what's going on."

"B..but you're so busy. I can't take up your time. And I'm not even allowed out," I falter.

"It's fine, you're with me. I'm not going to let you do anything, they know that. And you're not taking up my time. I'm on my break. I can spend it however I want."

Meg takes me downstairs, stopping only to get herself a hot chocolate from the vending machine. She offers me one too, but unsurprisingly, I decline, because today, it's an effort for me to even drink water.

Hot chocolate in hand, she checks that my feed is running, takes me by the arm and walks with me out of the main doors and down the road to a park not far from the hospital.

"Sit", she says, gesturing to a nearby bench. "We've done enough walking for today already. Tell me what's going on, please."

I do as she says, trying unsuccessfully to compose myself before working out how to put what I'm feeling into words in a way that might make some sort of sense.

"I just…I just don't know what to do. Everything they said was awful and I feel so judged and scrutinised and like, misunderstood. I might as well have been speaking a totally different language."

I'm crying harder now, so much that my last few words are barely audible through all the sobbing and I'm embarrassed at myself for getting so upset.

"I'm so sorry," Meg says gently. "Can I hug you? I was just going to do it but I thought I should probably ask in case you didn't want me to."

When I nod, she pulls me close to her, my tears dampening the fabric of her coat.

"You're lucky this is waterproof, otherwise you'd be very soggy by now", I say with an apologetic smile.

"And I'm the one who should be sorry. I'm sure this isn't exactly how you wanted to be spending your lunch break, especially when you hardly ever get the chance to take one."

"I already told you. It's my lunch break and I can spend it however I want, so today I'm choosing to spend it with you," she says, smiling at me and taking a sip of her hot chocolate.

For the next 15 minutes, Meg holds me close to her and listens as I cry and tell her the ins and outs of my shambolic Ward Round.

"It's just so frustrating", I say, tears rolling thick and fast down my face. "I tried to explain how I feel, and how I can't cope in this body, and in my head, but none of them were listening. They just kept talking about all the self harm as if I'm doing it on purpose, and how I'm not making any progress, and *then* they threatened to send me to an acute unit as though that's the solution to everything. I don't understand where they're coming from, or how any of this is even logical. It's like they think sending me to a psych ward will make my eating disorder magically disappear when they must *know* I wouldn't eat a thing. It'd be the quickest relapse imaginable. It's so, so horrible. I feel so lost and alone and miserable. I'm trying as hard as I can to cope but they just don't seem to recognise any of it. I feel like such a failure."

"I'm so sorry you feel like this," Meg says. "And I don't know for sure because I wasn't there, but you're right, it doesn't make any sense. I'm sure they're just worried and they're probably working out the best thing to do but I know it doesn't feel like that. I hate seeing you so upset, it breaks my heart. I wish there was more I could do."

Meg finishes the last of her hot chocolate and gets up to put the empty cup in the bin before bending down to give me another hug.

"Honestly, you've done more than enough," I tell her. "Just taking me away from that place and listening to me without judging or questioning me, that means so much. If you hadn't found me when you did I don't know what I'd have done. Probably proved them all right and got myself sent to an acute unit."

"I know, and that's the last thing I want for you. Taking all of this out on yourself won't solve anything, and you're such a lovely person, you don't deserve any of this. I just wish I could take it all away for you," she says, giving me an empathetic smile.

She looks at her watch, gestures to the park gates and we take a slow walk back to the hospital in comfortable silence - an unspoken agreement that, even if only for a brief moment, things are okay. Before we go inside, she looks at me, gives me one last hug and says,

"I know things are really hard, and I know you don't feel heard. I'm sorry today has been so difficult. But I'm here, and I'm listening, whenever you need to talk - even if all you want to do is cry. And although it doesn't feel like it now, things *will* get better. I promise you, they will."

I've often heard the phrase, 'the smallest act of kindness can save a life', and in that moment, I realise quite how true it is. I hope Meg realises it, too.

Chapter 15
Church Pew Juice

According to the calendar, it's supposed to be the first day of Spring, but the weather outside is grim, and almost everyone on the unit has come down with a horrible cold. People are coughing and sneezing all over the place, and lateral flow tests are being handed out the way I imagine gas masks were at the start of WWII.

Although none of us have Covid (yet), the whole situation is taking me right back to the surreal, topsy-turvy horror of the first lockdown. It's like March 2020 all over again, except I'm stuck in an EDU being force-fed, and I'm not even allowed in the garden.

Some of us are in the lounge laying on the sofas, coughing and groaning like Victorian waifs who've been struck down by Consumption. It's in moments like this that anorexia is particularly loud, berating me for being useless and lazy, and of course, for having breakfast. Even though I know it's 'normal', and practically everyone in the world will be doing the same thing, my mind has turned this information on its head. The guilt is so intense that I feel as though I've just killed a small child with my bare hands, not eaten a banana and a bowl of Weetabix.

In the corner of the room, Natalie is hunched over, nose buried in a bundle of tissues, and her face bright red from the effort of coughing. She offers me some Olbas Oil which I gratefully accept, hobbling over to her with the zeal of an OAP, and sprinkling it liberally onto my own wad of Kleenex.

"Come to the kitchen," she whispers, her voice groggy and full of cold. "I've got something that will heal us both!"

I follow her, all the while wondering whether she's about to offer me a concoction of herbs, or some sort of New Age, hemp-infused elixir of life.

Opening her locker and moving aside the jars of almond butter, cacao powder and Deliciously Ella 'superfood granola', she reaches for a small glass bottle labelled 'Organic elderberry syrup.'

"Forgive me if I'm stating the obvious, but what is it?" I ask suspiciously, reluctant to try anything that might make me feel worse than I already do.

"Honestly, I don't really know," Natalie says, her face breaking into a grin.

"I just got it from the health food shop in town, and it's meant to be good for colds. Get some of it down you. I've had tons already today and I reckon I feel better."

As she takes a spoon out of the cutlery drawer, pours a big glug of it and points it right at me, I can't help but feel as though I'm being initiated into some sort of cult.

"Hmmm. I don't know if I trust it. What does it taste like?" I ask, not sure whether my hesitation is driven by the anorexia, or simply because what she's offering me looks a bit weird.

"Err…sort of sweet and a bit herbal-y. It's actually quite nice."

I stare down at the spoonful of dark purple syrup and rationalise that since it's the colour of crushed up blackberries, it surely can't be that bad, so I brace myself and let her put the spoon into my mouth, as though I'm a toddler with a tummy ache lapping up Calpol.

As soon as it hits my taste buds, I wince involuntarily, and look at her in wild indignation.

"That," I gasp, swallowing with difficulty, "is disgusting. I don't know how you can drink it."

"Really?!" She exclaims, laughing and looking genuinely surprised. "I like it. It just tastes a bit medicinal, that's all."

"Medicinal? It absolutely doesn't. It tastes like…like a church. That smell you get when you walk into a church and sit down on one of the pews. That's what it tastes like. A church pew! It's awful!"

As I say this, I notice that Natalie is looking at me as though I've gone insane, and in hindsight, I think she's probably right.

"A church pew?! When have you ever tasted one of those?" She laughs, pouring herself another generous spoonful.

"Well, I haven't, obviously, but it just tastes exactly how they smell. A mix of dust, incense, mahogany, and lots of old bodies," I say triumphantly, feeling pretty pleased at the accuracy - and detail - of my description.

"I take it you're not a fan then?"

"Actually," I ask, unable to believe what I'm about to say, "Can I have some more? I think it's addictive."

She bursts out laughing, and then says, "Of course. You can have as much as you like. The expression on your face when you drink it is amazing. Honestly, it's quite literally made my day."

Since then, this syrup, which both of us now affectionately call 'church pew juice', has become a bit of a cure-all remedy, and our saving grace. If in doubt, we just neck a spoonful or two of the stuff, and wait for it to work its magic.

Chapter 16

Mary, I'm Dying

Mary is the ward OT, and she's a very lovely lady, but when it comes to emotional support, she's about as useful as a chocolate teapot. Each week in Ward Round, she's asked to give the MDT some feedback from the OT side of things, and every time, without fail, her contributions are so blithe and whimsical that I find myself struggling not to laugh out loud. About a month or so ago, after I'd just spent 15 minutes telling the consultant that I didn't want any nutrition and just wanted to die, Mary chipped in with an update that was so wonderfully irrelevant that it actually stopped me in my tracks and almost made me want to laugh. Although not completely gone, any suicidal ideation I had was put on pause, while I tried to register exactly what this woman had said.

The discussion in the room had gone from the fact that I wasn't allowed to have baths unsupervised in case I decided to try and drown myself, to:

"Yes, well, Sophia has been decorating a 'self-soothe box' during her 1:1 sessions, so, um…yes. That seems to be going well. Maybe next week we can start thinking about what she might like to put in it. That would, um, be a really, um…positive step forward."

I've heard from several other patients that Mary also has a miraculous habit of pouncing on people at the most inopportune moments, like when they're in the midst of a rolling panic attack, or are just about to faint, and although I'm yet to experience this myself, I can only imagine how jarring it must be.

On one particular occasion, she opened a patient's bedroom door to find them laying on the floor in 'child pose', crying their eyes out and hyperventilating, clearly in the middle of a very bad panic episode. Upon seeing this, Mary failed to register the gravity of the situation, simply smiling down at them before asking whether they'd like to make a wrap or a jacket potato as part of her afternoon cooking group. After a few minutes, the patient forced themselves up into a sitting position, stared up at her with tears in their eyes, and shouted, "Mary, I can't make a wrap, or a potato. I'm dying."

17

Rock Bottom Has
A Basement

*"The best bit about rock bottom is the rock part.
You discover the solid bit of you. The bit that can't
be broken down further. The thing you might
sentimentally call a soul. At our lowest, we
find the solid ground of our foundation.
And we can build ourselves anew."*
– Matt Haig

I'm in the MDT room with the consultant having
our weekly 1:1 catch-up, which makes it sound a
lot more casual than it really is. Together with Ward
Round, this 'catch-up' is something I tend to spend a

large proportion of my time dreading. If given the choice, I think I'd much rather be locked in a cage with a sabre-tooth tiger than have a meeting with the consultant to talk about my feelings and how I think my treatment is going. But as with most things that happen on the ward, I don't really have a choice, so I sit down opposite Dr Q, and brace myself for what might be coming next.

"So," she says brightly, looking at me in a way that suggests she can see right into my soul. "How are you doing?"

"I hate this," I blurt out angrily, doing everything I can to avoid bursting into tears.

Dr Q is silent, and as she waits for me to continue, her eyes widen with intrigue and curiosity.

"I hate this. All of it. I don't want any of it. I can't do this anymore. I don't want to be here," I say, my voice wobbling as my eyes fill with tears. I try unsuccessfully to blink them away, and feel my face begin to redden as they roll down my cheeks, splashing all the way down onto the grey carpeted floor.

For some reason, I'm overcome with a mixture of embarrassment and shame so intense it's as if I were sitting in front of her completely naked. This woman knows almost everything about me, and yet I can't bear the thought of her seeing me cry.

"Hmm," she says, neither gently nor unkindly, and I can tell she's about to ask me a question I won't want to answer.

"When you say you can't do this anymore, what do you mean? The treatment, your meal plan, what is it?" she asks, passing me a tissue.

"All of it," I mumble, trying not to show how frustrated I am - both at myself, and at how much she doesn't seem to understand.

"Hmm," she says again. "And when you say you don't want to be here, do you mean here in the hospital?"

"Anywhere," I reply bluntly. "I don't want to be anywhere. All I want is to disappear." I'm crying harder now, in spite of myself, and I have to blink furiously just to be able to see her face through my tears.

"Hmm," she says again, sounding more intrigued than ever now, which makes me feel less like a person with an eating disorder, and more like a lab rat that's being scrutinised as part of some sort of weird experiment.

There's another long pause, and then, before I can stop myself, I say,

"I don't want to eat. I don't want anything. I just want to be left alone."

"So, are you saying you want to starve yourself to death?" she asks, her tone as casual as if we were talking about the weather.

"I just don't want any nutrition. I don't want anything. Just let me go. Please." By now, I'm crying so much it's a wonder I don't drown myself in a pool of my own tears, and it's a while before I realise that I'm shouting.

The Consultant is silent again, this time for so long that I start to wonder whether she's forgotten how to speak. I don't have a watch and there's no clock in the room, but it feels like we've been sitting here for a decade.

When she finally speaks, Dr Q looks deep into my eyes and asks,

"Do you want to die?"

Although really, I knew it was coming, her question catches me off guard and I have to think for a few minutes before attempting to put what I'm feeling into words.

"N..no," I falter, my words slow and deliberate. "It's not that I want to die. I've never really thought about dying. Like, the *act* of dying. I just don't want to be alive if it means feeling like this. And from where I'm sitting, I just can't see a way out. I...I can't do this anymore."

SOPHIA PURCELL

"I'm sorry things are so difficult," she says after a while, her voice much gentler now than I've ever heard it before. "I can't do anything to change how you feel, and I definitely can't let you go home and waste away to nothing, but I want you to know something."

I look at her blankly, unsure of what she's going to say, my eyes still full of tears.

"I was thinking about you earlier, and I just had this vision of you in a much better place. You were doing your counselling and helping people, and you were well and so much happier. I could see it all, and I really do believe you'll get there. And all I can say is that I have a lot of respect for you right now. A *lot* of respect. This might feel like rock bottom, but it won't last forever."

At this point, I feel I ought to say something meaningful, but I don't have the words, so I just fix my gaze intently on the floor.

"This might feel like rock bottom, but gradually, if you give it time, these feelings will pass and things won't seem so bad anymore," she says again, the look in her eyes much softer now.

What she says genuinely touches me, and I know I ought to thank her, but my dark sense of humour kicks in instead, and before I can stop myself, I say,

"Ah, I don't know Dr Q. I wouldn't want to speak too soon. I've heard rock bottom has a basement."

18

The Things You Do for Love

I t's 5.30pm on a Tuesday, and I am preparing to go to war with half a jacket potato (believe it or not, that isn't the most ridiculous thing I've ever written down on paper).

Apart from yoghurt and Weetabix, this will be the first solid food that's passed my lips in over six months, so it's safe to say I'm absolutely terrified. Rationally, I know it's not going to hurt me, because, at the end of the day, it's just a potato, and the sensible part of me knows the worst thing that could possibly happen is that I'll feel a bit full.

So I want to make it clear that it isn't the potato I'm scared of, but rather, the *idea* of the potato, and everything it represents. I know I probably sound crazy - and maybe I am - but to me, this meal is so much more than a bog standard Maris Piper with a few baked beans on top. This potato - and most significantly - *eating* this potato, is a symbol of greed, weakness, worthlessness, failure, and so much more besides.

I shouldn't be overthinking it, but my mind has gone into overdrive, and no matter which way I look at it, I seem to be in a lose-lose situation. If I eat the potato, the anorexia in me will be livid, tearing me down for giving in, losing control, and just generally being the most terrible person alive. But if I *don't* eat the potato, the non-anorexic part of me - however small - will be distraught, and I'll have failed all over again.

A few nights ago, I was talking to some of the other girls about the prospect of eating this potato, and Natalie asked me if there was anything she could do that would help. Instantly, I said no. The way I saw it, there was absolutely nothing in the world that could make this any easier, other than, you know, not having to eat it.

"There must be something though, surely. Just name it and I'll do it - within reason," she says, flashing me a wicked grin.

"Honestly Nat, I can't think of anything. I just can't do it. I feel so disgusting," I tell her, deflated and defeated, but also angry at how pathetic I sound.

"You can. You can, and you absolutely will. And most importantly, you *aren't* disgusting. We'll do it together, that way you won't be on your own. And if you think of anything at all in the meantime that'll make it easier for you, I'll do it," she says gently, taking my hand and clasping it in both of hers.

In that moment, her kindness warms my heart, and it's an effort to stop myself from crying.

Natalie gets up to leave, her lips breaking into a familiar mischievous smile.

"Honestly, if there's anything - absolutely anything - you just name it and I'll do it. If it'll help, I'll even dress up as a jacket potato. I bet they sell costumes on Amazon."

At 5.45, the potato arrives, and I sit down in front of it feeling like a prisoner headed for the gallows. Every fibre of my being is screaming at me not to do it - to throw the god-forsaken thing in the bin (or better, at the wall), retreat to the safety of my bed, and never do so much as think about another potato as long as I live.

As I stare at it, willing it to disappear, my mind wanders and I begin picturing all the other people who might be sitting down to a jacket potato at this very same moment, probably picking up their knife and fork without experiencing even an ounce of guilt.

"How do they do it?" I think to myself. "Imagine just being able to eat when you're hungry and stop when you're full, without feeling as though your entire world is crumbling at your feet. Imagine that."

After a few minutes, there's a knock at my door, and because I'm so on edge, I can't help but flinch at the unexpected noise.

"Hello?" I say tentatively, more of a question than a greeting.

The door opens, and in walks Natalie, her whole body obscured by a beige-coloured blob with brown flecks all over it, and a small round hole through which only her face is visible.

I look at her in disbelief, my eyes scanning from her head to her feet and back again, and in spite of myself, I can't help but laugh.

"What the hell? What the fuck are you wearing?!" I ask, not quite able to believe what I'm seeing.

"I'm a jacket potato - obviously. I come in peace, and I'm here to assist with all your potato needs," she laughs, grinning from ear to ear.

"Where did you get that from?" I ask.

"Amazon. I told you I'd do it. It's the best £22 I've ever spent. How do I look?" she asks, waddling over to the mirror to take a proper look at herself.

"You look fucking mental. I love it," I tell her, doubling over in a fit of giggles.

"Is it helping? Look, I'll even dance for you. Put some music on."

"You know what, it actually is. Every bit of me wants to cry, but whenever I look at you, it's just impossible. I can't believe you actually did it."

"Told you I would, didn't I? I even tried to get some baked bean leggings, but they wouldn't have arrived in time so this'll have to do."

For the next half an hour, Natalie dances around my room in her potato costume to 'Temperature' by Sean Paul, shouting, "You've got this! Potato believes in you!" and in between fits of laughter, I do my best to finish the real jacket potato.

When I'm done, she lets out a long breath, pulls the costume up over her head, and throws it onto my bed.

"Where did it all go wrong, eh?" she asks. "I'm 33 years old and I'm trapped in a psychiatric hospital, dancing around in a jacket potato costume while all my friends are out there getting married and having babies. Oh the things you do for love."

"Honestly," I say, tears of laughter now streaming down my face, "I really don't know. But all I can say is you're amazing, and this is one of the nicest things anyone has ever done for me."

I've often wondered what constitutes true love, and now I think I've found out: a friend who dances around dressed as a jacket potato, just to help you eat your dinner.

19

A Quiet Revolution

"I am loving myself out of the dark"
– Rupi Kaur

In the recovery community, especially Instagram, there's a lot of talk about tolerating your body. Usually, this is meant positively, in the sense of managing your own expectations, and not pushing yourself to achieve the 'perfect' kind of recovery (whatever that means).

Scrolling through my Instagram feed, I've come across hundreds of posts that talk about how it's totally okay not to love, or even like your body, but simply to get to a place where you can tolerate it just enough to live the life you ultimately want to live.

As someone who's always had a difficult relationship with their body, I've been thinking about this a lot. At first, the idea gave me a sense of reassurance, because loving - or even liking - my body was something I never thought I could achieve. But lately, I've had a change of heart.

After six months in hospital, I am fully weight-restored (again), and if I'm completely honest, I hate it. I hate the way my body looks, I hate the way my clothes fit, and most of all, I hate the way it feels. That said, I've gradually come to realise that carrying around all this hate is as pointless as it is painful. I've spent the past 13 years of my life trying to change, manipulate, starve, punish and shrink it, and it hasn't got me anywhere. Really and truly, I destroyed my body for a peace of mind that never came.

As much as I might not like it, this is the only body I will ever have, and in spite of everything I've put it through, it's carried me this far in life. But when it comes to loving my body, the prospect still makes me cringe. How can I ever love something that feels so uncomfortable and so totally and utterly wrong?

The counselling diploma I'm studying has led me to think more deeply about my place in the world, the different aspects of my life, the things I love, and the things I don't. I love my family, I love my friends, I love my cat, I love writing, I love that I'm trainee counsellor, and many more things besides.

Why, then, can't I love my body?

The answer is, I have to. Or at least, I have to learn to try.

So, I'm starting a quiet revolution. Instead of simply putting up with, and tolerating my body, I'm going to try my best to learn to love it - starting by taking better care of it.

I've bought clothes that fit my new shape - the shape I have resisted for 13 years - products that will help me look after my feet, skin and hair, and yesterday, I got a massage for the first time in years. In the past, this was something I would *never* have allowed myself to do, simply because it felt so unnecessary, and like something I did not deserve. But you know what, I actually loved it, and afterwards, I felt the most relaxed I think I ever have. It was as though my whole body was letting out a sigh of relief, thanking me for finally giving it the care and attention it so desperately needs.

20

The Footprints in The Sand

It is dinner time again, and I am staring down at a bowl of spotted dick and custard.

To say that I am overwhelmed would be a gross understatement. In my mind, the cake and custard seem to have undergone some sort of twisted and miraculous transformation. Instead of being a harmless - and probably quite enjoyable - end to an evening meal, the pudding in front of me represents a multitude of horrible, terrible, impossible things. The spotted dick is a potent symbol of everything I have ever hated about myself. It represents failure, greed, weakness, laziness, defeat, worthlessness, gluttony, selfishness, inadequacy, and so, so much more besides. In my mind, this pudding exists only as an impossibility, sort of like climbing Mount Everest with two broken legs.

I know that I should pick up the spoon and eat what is in front of me. After all, that is what I've come here to do. But I just can't.

I feel depleted, exhausted, totally and utterly drained, just as I did in the days before I was admitted to hospital. This doesn't make sense. My physical reserves have been restored. Maybe not fully, but certainly enough to keep my brain and body functioning better than they have been for a while. So why do I feel this way all over again? Why does it feel like my mind is on fire? Why can't I just keep going?

Sitting opposite me across the dining table, is a member of staff. Someone who, during the course of my time on the ward, I have come to know and trust. As always, she is firm. She won't stand for any nonsense - especially not when "it's the anorexia talking". But she is also fair. She can see when someone is trying, and today is no exception. Letting out a long sigh, she takes away the pudding and replaces it with a cup of Fortisip.

For the next half an hour, she coaxes me through, and, in spite of myself, and in spite of all the tears, I drink it, right down to the very last drop, even though every ounce of my being is willing me to do the opposite.

When I am done, she takes my hand, looks me in the eye, and says,

"I know how hard that was, but you did it. And I know you want to give up. I know you don't believe in yourself, but I believe in you - we all do. Sometimes, when you feel like giving up, what you need is for someone else to support you, to carry you, until you're strong enough to do it for yourself."

I look back at her and I want to say something, but I seem to have forgotten how to speak.

"Have you ever heard of 'The Footprints in the Sand'?" she asks.

"No," I say slowly, unsure how relevant this is going to be.

"Well, it's from The Bible. I don't know it word for word, but I'll give you the jist of it:

One night, a man is walking along a beach, talking to God. He's been walking a long way, and when he looks behind him to see how far he has come, he sees two sets of footprints in the sand, as though two people had been walking along beside one another.

When he looks more closely, he sees that for part of the way, only one set of footprints are visible in the sand. This makes him angry, because he has endured a lot of pain and anguish on his journey and he feels as though he's been let down.

So, he asks God a question:

'Why, when you knew I was suffering, were you not always there by my side? Why did you abandon me when I needed you?'

'I never once left your side,' God says to the man.

'On the journey, there were moments when the pain became too much for you to bear. You see only one set of footprints in the sand because that was when I picked you up, and I carried you, until you had the strength to walk on your own.'"

When she's finished telling the story, the member of staff looks at me and says:

"That's what we're all here for, and if you need us to, that's what we'll do. Things might feel hopeless now, but I promise you, it won't always be this way. We will carry you until you're ready to do it on your own. You might not think you're worth it, but we really, really do."

Chapter 21

Lovely

"**G**ood morning my dear," one of the staff says enthusiastically, standing half in the doorway, half out of it. "I'm just going down to get your porridge from the kitchen."

I stare back at her, blankly, by now resigned to my fate, begrudgingly coming to terms with my newfound identity as 'a person who eats breakfast.'

"Thank you," I say, briefly meeting her gaze before looking intently down at the carpet.

"You look lovely," she says brightly, glancing from my head down to my boots and back again. The way she puts it, I can tell there's no room for objection or debate. It is, purely and simply, a statement of fact.

"Oh, thanks," I mumble, caught slightly off guard. This does not go unnoticed.

"I don't feel lovely. I feel like a whale," I say before I can stop myself, bracing myself for her response.

"Yes but you know that's your eating disorder talking, don't you? And it's utter nonsense. You're a young woman. Young women are supposed to look like young women, not six year old boys."

"We need to stand up to this ideal and show the world what *real* women look like. Real women have curves and bums and boobs and they eat their porridge. Come on, let's go!"

Chapter 22

Dance Me Through the Panic

This is a diary entry that I wrote sometime in 2018, when I first started treatment for anorexia. It's not specifically related to my inpatient journey, but it tells something of the story of how my eating disorder began, so it only felt right to include it.

> *"Dance me through the panic,*
> *'til I'm gathered safely in".*
> – Leonard Cohen

It's a Thursday evening at the end of September and I am sitting at the kitchen table staring out of the window, when it dawns on me that I am scared of everything.

I'm scared of new faces. Of not being good enough. Of being myself. Of not knowing who that is. I'm scared of being alone. Of being in crowded places. Of being too loud or too quiet. I'm scared of my body, even though it's my own. I'm scared of taking up space.

Today, for the first time in my life, I'm also scared of pizza. Specifically, the pizza that's sitting on the plate in front of me going cold and congealed and crispy. I've never been frightened of food before, and it's a new and interesting sensation. It's also horrible.

I'm so preoccupied by the pizza and my new found fear of absolutely everything, that I don't notice you enter the room. Nor do I hear your footsteps as you walk up beside me to place a hand on my shoulder.

I feel the weight of it, heavy and yet somehow gentle, the subtle force an early indication of just how powerful you'll come to be.

I try shaking you off, just a little (you're a stranger after all), and your grip tightens instantly. A warning.

In that moment, the space between 'doing' and 'not doing' shrinks. Possibility and opportunity close in on one another, but so too, I notice, does fear. Chaos has been replaced by certainty and calm, and for now at least, I don't even have to think. Whenever something goes wrong, you are there by my side with an answer to my call of distress.

At first, your 'solutions' don't make much sense. Some days, it all seems ridiculous, and I question whether you really know what you're doing. How on earth, I think to myself, will skipping breakfast help me speak my mind, instead of letting other people's voices drown out my own? If I survive on sips of fizzy drinks, will I really be able to walk into a room without flinching at every touch, or wanting the ground to swallow me whole? What does emptiness have to do with anything at all?

"Emptiness makes everything easier," you say. "It cuts through the chaos."

And so, I listen. I listen because I'm scared and alone. I listen because I don't know what else to do.

Slowly but surely, I begin to understand how it works, and it's not long before I see the world exactly as you do. Day by day, your words become thoughts and those thoughts become actions.

I start to prioritise lightness over lazy mornings in bed, emptiness over laughter and cake. I mistake self-denial for self-control, and it's not fun, but it does make things easier. You weren't wrong about that.

Taking my hand, you dance me through the panic 'til I'm gathered safely in, like in that song by Leonard Cohen. On good days, I feel safe, on better ones I feel invincible, and it's all because of you.

But I don't recall those lyrics then. On that Thursday at the end of September, I am nineteen. I wear too much black, and too much eyeliner, and I'm obsessed with Panic! At the Disco. When you first come into my life, I don't even know who Leonard Cohen is.

It's not until years later, when I've carried you with me through four university degrees, into countless office jobs and across four different continents, that I finally make the link.

Years later, I'm sitting in a lecture theatre having retreated back into education with the proverbial tail between my legs, listening to a symposium on Trauma, Attachment Theory and 'The Vulnerable Child'.

After talking at length about Bowlby and Harlow, Lorenz and Emmerson, the Professor giving the lecture finishes with a YouTube clip, which she says, perfectly sums up the relationship between the teacher and the vulnerable child.

"The vulnerable child is scared, lonely and frightened", she says. "They need someone to take them by the hand, to tell them that it really is okay to feel, and at times, to behave the way they do. All they are doing is finding a way to cope."

With that, the lecture ends, the music starts to play, and the black and white stills fill the screen: 'Dance me to the end of love', by Leonard Cohen. And that, I think, is when it clicked. Slowly at first, and then all at once. For the first time, I understood why you came into my world, and why I let you stay for so long.

For better or worse, life is chaos. It's messy and awful and wonderful and then awful again. It's love, heartbreak, joy, pain and panic. And for all these years, you have been the one dancing me through, gathering me safely in.

Except that it's not safe, not really. I know that now, and I am trying so hard to believe it. I am trying to unlearn everything you taught me, one step at a time.

Chapter 23

Do It Tomorrow

"Sometimes, I look at my scars and I wish they weren't there. Other times, I look at my scars and see something else: a girl who was trying to cope with something horrible that she should never have had to live through at all. My scars show pain and suffering, but they also show my will to survive. They're part of my history that'll always be there."
– Cheryl Rainfield

Over the past 10 or so years, I've struggled a lot with self harm. Whenever I think about this, I always tell myself that it's never been that bad, because unlike some people, I haven't been in and out of A&E, and, until recently, never required much medical treatment. But that's the thing. I'm not comparing myself to anyone else, I'm comparing myself to me; specifically, the little me who would never have dreamed of punishing herself or intentionally causing herself pain, and who, for years, didn't even know what self harm was. So when I think about it like that, it has been - and still is - a pretty big deal.

Because my eating disorder has a lot to do with self harm and self punishment, my urges tend to become particularly strong whenever my other coping mechanisms are taken away - namely, when I'm unable to over-exercise or restrict what I eat. So, since being in hospital, my self harm urges and episodes have increased dramatically.

Of course, this isn't something I'm proud of. Really and truly, I don't even like talking about it, and if I could keep my wounds hidden from the rest of the world forever, I absolutely would. But when you're in hospital, that isn't really an option, and over the past year and a half, I've been forced to reveal and confront parts of myself that I never thought I would. Parts of myself I didn't even want to admit were there. But I always wanted this book to be an accurate and truthful depiction of my inpatient journey, so if I didn't talk about this, I'd be leaving out a huge aspect of my story.

Although I've obviously had good times and bad times throughout the past 10 years, self harm is something I still struggle with a lot. I battle urges on a daily basis, and while acting on them does grant me some immediate relief, ultimately I know this is only temporary, just as the pain I feel - the pain that causes me to do it - is only temporary, and will pass in time as things always do. So, I'm not here to offer any advice, or to claim I've found some sort of miracle cure that has taken all my pain away, I'm just being honest about my struggles, in the hope that it might encourage anyone else who may be going through similar things to open up and seek help as well.

As I say, I don't have a miracle cure (although I really wish I did), but recently, I came across something that, I think, has helped me quite a lot, and with any luck, it might help you, too.

A friend sent me a video, from Tik Tok of all places, that really changed my way of thinking, and in all honesty, it actually made me cry (I've included a link to it in the 'Resources' section at the back of this book for anyone that might find it helpful, but for now, I'll just give you the gist of it).

In the video, a girl is talking about how she overcame her struggles, and has managed to stay self harm free for years. For her, as for me, self harm was very closely linked to her eating disorder; a way of coping, yes, but more than anything, a form of self punishment.

She tells the story of how she was in hospital, wanting more than anything to self harm, when a nurse asked her why she felt she needed to do it 'right now.' She listed all the reasons, and all the feelings that were making her urges so strong, and at the end of it all, the nurse responded by saying that in spite of all that, she still hadn't answered her question: the question of why she needed to do it 'right now.' Confused, she listed all her feelings again, unable to understand why the nurse couldn't see where she was coming from, and even then, the woman said she *still* hadn't answered her question. The reasons and feelings were there, without a doubt, but none of them explained why self harming 'right now' was the only viable option.

"So," the nurse said, "wait until tomorrow. Just go 24 hours without self harming, but tell yourself you can do it tomorrow."

At this point, the girl was confused.

"Wait, so you're saying I shouldn't self harm now, but you'll let me do it tomorrow?" she asked.

"Yes. Just wait 24 hours, and do it tomorrow."

Twenty-four hours pass and the girl manages to refrain from self harming, all on the promise that she can 'do it tomorrow.' The next day comes, her urges are still there, as strong as ever, and when the nurse returns, she says,

"It's been 24 hours. Can I self harm now?"

The nurse looks her in the eye and says,

"You've gone 24 hours without self harming. You've lasted that long, and that's a really big achievement. But if you've managed 24 hours, you can go another 24. Do it tomorrow."

At the end of the video, the girl says she lived by that mantra religiously for months, always telling herself when the urges were really, really strong, that if she just waited 24 hours, she could do it tomorrow. And that little mantra has helped her to stay self harm free for seven years.

Of course, this won't work for everyone, and even if it does, there will inevitably be times when the urges are just too overpowering, but for me, it really resonated. So now, every time I hear Paul's voice in my head and get the urge to self harm, I do my best to wait, all on the promise that I can do it tomorrow.

Chapter 24

Art Therapy Saved My Life

"No matter how dark it gets, the light
is always on its way"
– Rupi Kaur

"Who wants to come to art therapy?" Rhianne, one of the assistant psychologists asks, scanning around the lounge for willing participants.

When no one responds, she continues, as though letting us know exactly what we're in for will somehow make the prospect more appealing.

"It's not gonna be a proper session because Jenny, the *actual* Art Therapist, is on annual leave, but I can take you guys down to the room and you can just do your thing. I can't promise it'll be amazing, because I'm not gonna lie, I've never done art therapy in my life, but I'll put some tunes on and we can all just go for the vibes."

On this particular day, my mood is very, very low; the lowest it's been in a long, long time. Anorexia is screaming at me simply for existing, and daring to take up any space at all, and I can't imagine any kind of future for myself outside of this awful, insidious illness. Quite honestly, vibes or no vibes, I don't want to go to art therapy, I just want to die.

Of course, I don't tell Rhianne - or anyone - this. I just allow myself to be dragged along simply because it feels like too much effort to explain what's happening in my head, or why I don't want to go.

On the way down to the art room on the ground floor of the hospital, my mind runs away with itself and I start thinking about all the possible ways I could put an end to the torment I'm feeling.

The first thing that pops into my head is an overdose, because that seems like the cleanest and least painful way out, but obviously all the drugs are kept locked away in the clinic room, and the chances of me being able to sneak any into my bedroom are very, very slim, so that option is ruled out completely.

Next, I glance out of the window at all the cars sitting stationary in the car park, and wonder whether I could do a runner out into the main road and throw myself in front of the next oncoming vehicle. But yet again, practicality puts a stop to that idea. First of all, I'm on 1:1, which means there's someone watching my every move *all* the time, and secondly, I can't actually run, so even if I managed to get out of the hospital, someone would catch up with me in less than a minute.

My only option, it seems, would be to get hold of a knife or some other sharp object, although even this is just as far-fetched, because not only do I have no way of getting my hands on such a thing, my 1:1 would surely stop me before I managed to do so much as give myself a scratch the size and depth of a papercut. Still, my head refuses to give up, and I spend the first 15 minutes of 'art therapy' coming up with method after futile method, until Rhianne interrupts my morbid stream of consciousness by asking me a question.

"Soph, Jenny told me you've been making a 'self box.' Do you mind if I have a look at it? I'm really intrigued. I know you're not quite finished, but she said it's really beautiful."

"Er…sure," I say, clearly very distracted, getting up to take the wooden box down from one of the shelves and opening it for her to have a look.

"Oh my God! This is incredible!" she exclaims, casting her eyes over its Alice in Wonderland themed contents. "How did you even come up with that?"

"I dunno, I just really like books and writing and stuff. It's got a lot of my favourite quotes in it," I say, my tone of voice as flat as my mood.

"Honestly, it's so, so good. Do you mind if I show the others and then you can tell everyone a little bit about it - if that's okay with you," she adds gently, obviously taking note of the reluctance on my face.

As she passes my box around the room for everyone to look at, she turns Spotify on and begins searching for an art therapy style playlist.

"Before I just whack something on, do you guys have any requests? I'm not really sure what's appropriate. We definitely need something arty, but I don't wanna, y'know, kill the vibe," she says, laughing from beneath her mask.

At this point, Aliya, one of the loveliest and bubbliest HCAs on the ward, chimes in with the enthusiasm of a small child on a sugar high, "Nicki Minaj! *Please* put her new song on, Rhi. It's *such* a vibe, I love it!" she exclaims, her big brown eyes lighting up at the thought of it.

"Aliya, I don't care how much of a vibe you think it is, I'm *not* putting Nikki Minaj on during Art Therapy," Rhianne says in a disapproving tone, her professional psychologist hat firmly in place.

"Awww noooo Rhi. You *have* to. It's such a *tuneee!*" she says, almost pleading now, although it's obvious that the two of them are just messing around. If I had to choose one phrase to describe Aliya, I'd say she was like a ray of sunshine. Her smile just seems to light up the whole room, and as she's talking, I even find myself smiling too.

"No, I'm sorry Aliya, there'll be no Nikki Minaj today, at least not while we're in group. I've found a playlist called 'Relaxation and Contemplation.' I think that's *exactly* what we need," she says matter-of-factly, her voice full of mock professionalism.

"Oh Rhi, you're such a meanie. How can I possibly enjoy my watercolour painting without a bit of tuneage? If you put that relaxation stuff on, I'll probably just fall asleep and plonk my head down into all the paints," she says, laughing.

"Nope. Rhi is in professional therapist mode today, so relaxation it is. And anyway, you're not even meant to be painting, that's just for the patients", she says firmly, although once again, I can tell that she's only joking.

While all of this is going on, my box is being passed around the room, and people are staring down to examine its contents as though it's some sort of precious artefact you'd find in the British Museum, and I can't help but feel a little embarrassed. Cheeks reddening, my mind wanders again and I start scanning the room for any sharp objects, but of course, they've all been safely locked away.

When the last person has looked at the box, Rhianne passes it back to me and asks me to tell everyone what it's about. I wince involuntarily at the thought of this, feeling like a primary school child about to do 'show and tell,' but I do as I'm told, mainly out of sheer awkwardness.

"Well," I say slowly, "like Jenny said, it's a 'self box'. I really love books and quotes and reading, so I've decorated the inside with pages from Alice in Wonderland. I tea-stained and varnished them to make them look older, and I've put gold and copper foil around the edge of that illustration from The Mad Hatter's tea party. Then", I continue, getting into the swing of things, "I've included one of my favourite lines from a poem by Emily Dickinson, and stuck it underneath. The poem is very short, it goes like this:

> "Hope is the thing with feathers,
> That perches in the soul,
> And sings the song without the words,
> And never stops - at all."

"That's what the feathers are for," I say, pointing them out. "Then I've written some more of my favourite quotes and used tiny pegs to hang them all on a little washing line that goes around the edges. When it's finished, it'll have little bottles of glitter - they're meant to be a bit like treasure really - stuck on the inside, and a few other things I've collected, like shells and stones and some more feathers. Eventually, there's going to be handwritten quotes and poems all over the outside too, but I haven't got round to that yet. It's all a bit of a hotch-potch really," I say, my words starting to trail off.

"It doesn't look like a hotch-potch to me. It's beautiful. What's that round box in the middle, the one with the 'S' on it. Is there anything inside? Rhianne asks, clearly genuinely intrigued.

"Um, it's just a scroll with another of my favourite poems on it," I say, taking it out for her to have a proper look.

"Would you mind reading it to us?" she asks. "I'd really like to hear it from you."

"Er…sure," I say reluctantly. I clear my throat nervously, look down at the paper - even though I know the whole thing off by heart - and start to read aloud:

> "for the love of my life
> i am trying my best to have hope
> i'll keep greeting each morning
> with an *i will*
> when it feels like *i can't*
> i *will*
> i *will*
> i *will*
> meet a day that will melt me
> i *will* move
> and the sadness *will*
> fall off my shoulders
> to make room for joy

i *will* be full of colour
i *will* touch the sky again"
    – Rupi Kaur

When I've finished reading, I look around the room to see that everyone is beaming.

"That's so, so beautiful," Rhianne says, taking a long, deep breath. "Wow, I don't know about anyone else, but I'm actually starting to feel a little bit emotional."

"Me too," Aliya says, her eyes wet with a film of tears. "It's so hopeful and heartfelt, it really fits with the whole theme of your box."

"Yeah, totally," Rhianne agrees. "I know Jenny called it a 'self box', and I suppose it is, but to me it feels more like a hope box - something to keep you going when you feel like giving up."

As soon as she says this, the heaviness I'm feeling starts to lift a little and it's as though the dark clouds in my head have parted, letting in a small streak of sunlight, and with it, a tiny bit of hope.

I might not be happy, but for now, I don't want to die. And even though it's only for a very brief moment, I start to imagine what it would be like to be free.

Chapter 25

California Rocket Fuel

"A combination of mirtazapine and venlafaxine, known colloquially as California Rocket Fuel (CRF), sometimes used as a medication for treatment-resistant depression."

– Cambridge University Medical Journal

This morning in Ward Round, I found out that I've been on the wrong antidepressants for the last two weeks. After dropping that bombshell, the Consultant asked me how I felt, and if I'm completely honest, I was lost for words. I mean, how are you supposed to feel in that situation?

"It's definitely an error on our part, and we're just trying to work out how it's happened," she says, in a very serious tone.

"Fortunately, the two medications you've been on *can* be taken at the same time," she continues. "In fact, there are many people who find that the combination works really well for them. But in any case, this should still never have occurred, so I just want to apologise, and to let you know that you're completely within your rights to make a formal complaint, if that's something you'd like to do."

I stare blankly, looking from the Consultant to the GP, to the dietician, the psychologist, and back again, still at a loss for what to say.

"From what I understand, you weren't aware, so how are you feeling about it now that you know?" the Consultant asks again, a curious, but still very concerned look on her face.

"Honestly, this probably sounds stupid, but I really don't know. I think I just need a bit of time to process it," I say, speaking very slowly, as though I'm afraid of tripping over my own words.

"That's totally understandable. Think about it, and if you decide you want to take it further, we can help you to put that in motion."

"Thanks," I reply, still not entirely sure what I'm thanking her for: telling me they fucked up my medication, or offering to help me make a complaint.

I know I probably *should* complain, but right now, I can just about string a sentence together, let alone write a letter to the hospital director or the CQC.

In fact, the more I think about the situation, the worse it gets. I have a habit of catastrophizing even at the best of times, but when I'm presented with something like this, my brain just goes wild, coming up with all manner of terrible things that might have happened, and that might *still* happen.

"And how have you felt in yourself over the last two weeks?" the Consultant asks. "Have you noticed any difference, good *or* bad?"

"Well, considering I've been on two antidepressants, I haven't felt any happier at all. The only thing I've noticed is that I just can't cry. It's not as though I don't want to either. It's like I've got all this anger and sadness bubbling up inside of me, but no matter how hard I try, I've got no way of expressing it. Even now I probably look like I'm pretty relaxed, but in reality I feel like I'm going crazy. It's horrible."

"I can imagine," she says, even more serious than before. "That can't have been nice at all, and I'm so sorry it's happened. But as I said, this combination *can* be used together, and for some people, it's actually a very effective mood stabiliser."

"Yeah, maybe so, but not in my case, clearly. I just feel like I'm going to explode, but at the same time I know it won't happen. Like a bottle full of fizzy water with a cork that won't pop. Only without the sparkle, obviously."

"Hmmm," she says thoughtfully. "That *is* interesting."

"Is it? It seems pretty awful from where I'm sitting," I say sharply.

Her reply annoys me more than it should, not only because it detracts from the severity of the situation, but because for some unknown reason, that just seems to be her response to everything. No matter what you say, or how you say it, she always seems to respond with "*that's interesting….*"

And to someone from the outside, all of this might *well* be interesting, but if you're the one going through it, it's *far* from interesting. It's just a fucking nightmare.

"Well of course," she says, obviously trying to placate me, "and I don't want you to think we're denying that, or not taking it seriously, because we are. All I'm saying is that for me, it's just interesting to hear things from your point of view."

By the time she finishes speaking, her tone has softened a little, but even so, I can't help but feel like I've taken part in some weird trial experiment that's gone a bit wrong.

From the stony look on my face, she can tell this isn't going anywhere, so the Consultant brings the conversation back to her first point, this time with an expression so relaxed and breezy, you'd think we'd just been talking about the weather.

"Well, as I said before, you're perfectly entitled to make a complaint, so if you'd like to, just speak to the Ward Manager, and she'll get it sorted out for you."

Later that day, I bump into one of the other girls in the corridor, and in hushed tones, tell her all about what happened in my Ward Round.

"What the actual fuck?!" she says. "You've been on California Rocket Fuel for two weeks and no one even noticed? That's *so* bad. What are you gonna do?"

"I've no idea. They said I could make an official complaint if I want to, but I'm not sure I can be bothered. It'd probably ruffle a few feathers so I might wait until after I'm discharged."

"Yeah, good idea. But I'd *definitely* complain if I were you. That's so, *so* bad. Anything could have happened," she says, her voice full of intrigue and indignation. "That stuff's supposed to be insane. That's why they call it California Rocket fuel. I kind of wish it'd happened to me instead. I want to try it just to see what it's like. How do you feel?"

"You mean how did I feel while I was on it? Or how do I feel now?" I ask, still keeping my voice lowered.

"Well, both," she says, still seriously, but with the corners of her mouth turning upwards into the slightest hint of a smile.

"Bloody awful," I tell her dramatically. "I can't cry or get angry or anything, no matter how I'm feeling on the inside. I just feel really numb, a bit like a robot or something. Certainly not anything like I'm on rocket fuel! 100% would *not* recommend," I say, laughing at the sheer madness of our conversation.

"Oh God that's so shit. I'm so sorry. Maybe I don't want to try it after all. What did Dr Q say?"

"Nothing much. She had a serious look on her face, but really she was quite chill about it. All she kept saying was that it's a combination that's really effective for some people, and that I could make an official complaint if I wanted to. I don't know what to do. It's so fucking weird. I know it's an odd thing to say, but I feel a bit, like, violated, even though I know it was a mistake and no one did it on purpose."

"No, babe don't worry. It's not weird at all. I'd feel the same if I were you. It's like someone's been fucking around with your head - and your body - and you had no idea. It's so scary. Imagine if you'd tried to kill yourself or gone psychotic or something, like I did when they put me on that bloody fluoxetine," she says laughing.

"That's so true. I mean, obviously it hasn't been nice feeling like a robot with no emotions, but at least I didn't start thinking everyone in here was trying to do me in," I say, giving her a wry smile. "I guess you're just a bit crazier than I am, but that's not new. I knew it right from the first day I met you," I tell her playfully, blowing her a kiss as I make my way back to my room.

26

Covid Chaos

I don't know what's happening, or what day it is. All I know is that there's a fridge in the lounge and everyone is going home. Yesterday, we had a confirmed Covid case on the ward for the second time in three months, and as of this morning, four more people have tested positive, including one of the Consultants.

As you might imagine, the place is in utter chaos. People are scurrying around as though the apocalypse is coming, bathing in hand sanitiser and crying into their face masks, and the air is thick with a mixture of panic, dread, and of course, Covid.

Since many of us are triple vaccinated, the fear - I suspect - isn't so much about catching the virus, but more at the prospect of having to spend 10 whole days isolating in our bedrooms without being allowed to set so much as a single toe over the threshold. And even for those of us who are testing negative, the situation doesn't look much brighter.

After breakfast, the MDT called an emergency meeting to give us an update on the 'outbreak', as well as the hospital's current Covid-19 policy. Although, outside in the real world, most of the restrictions have been relaxed or removed altogether, inside these walls it's a totally different story. According to hospital policy, any more than two confirmed positive cases constitutes an outbreak, and with an outbreak comes lockdown. For all of us, this means no home leave and no time off the unit whatsoever - not even to the garden - until the last person has tested negative. This is where the real horror begins, because although at the moment, we're only looking at 10 days, if more and more people contract it, the whole saga could go on endlessly, and we'd all be stuck inside for months.

To make matters worse, the ward is in the process of being renovated, and the two dining rooms are being combined into one to make room for an extra lounge area. Ordinarily, this wouldn't be much of a problem, but right now, the last thing any of us need is a load of noise and more disruption on top of what is already a pretty shambolic situation.

Because of the renovation, both dining rooms are in total disarray. There's food and drink piled up in boxes all over the place, and all the white goods have been dumped unceremoniously into the lounge, so there's nowhere for any of us to even sit, let alone have any food. Again, in normal circumstances, this wouldn't be the end of the world, but given that this is an Eating Disorder Unit, in which all we're expected to do all day is eat and sit down, it's actually a pretty big deal.

If they haven't made a break for it already, most informal patients have packed up their things and headed off to isolate at home quicker than anyone can say 'Covid,' and to be honest, I don't blame them. No matter which way you look at it, if you're forced to spend 10 days inside, it'd be much more appealing to do this in your own home than to be stuck in a psych ward that currently looks like an episode of DIY SOS gone wrong. But those of us who are on a Section 3 - myself included - have no choice but to suck it up and stay put, which quite frankly, is absolutely terrifying.

Some of us ask if we, too, can isolate at home, but really, we know we haven't got a hope in hell and are only trying our luck. So we just sit in our rooms awaiting the next update, taking lateral flow test after lateral flow test, and hoping against hope that the dreaded second red line doesn't appear. Every time I do it, I feel less like an EDU patient, and more like a teenager holed up in the school toilets, anxiously awaiting the results of a pregnancy test.

Thankfully, I continue to test negative throughout the whole 'outbreak' and although that doesn't count for much given that we're all still *technically* in lockdown, I've never felt so lucky to be able to walk down a corridor, or go and make a cup of tea whenever I like. If this experience has taught me anything, it's to appreciate the little things, and to never take my - relative - freedom for granted ever again.

27

Lost In Translation

This is a diary entry written the week before I was admitted to an EDU for the second time in the autumn of 2022.

I walk out of the pharmacy onto the dirty, rubbish-laden pavement and realise that it's late afternoon; somehow, already the end of another school day.

Children are everywhere, or so it seems. Jackets hanging haphazardly off shoulders, book bags trailing through autumn leaves. Learning long-forgotten in favour of pre-teatime treats clutched tightly with both hands. Rosy-cheeked and full of chatter, their joy ought to be contagious; giggles and anticipation the currency of a Friday afternoon.

At the traffic lights, I wait for green and make my way back home, wanting nothing more than to be away from everything. And not in the ten minutes it will take to get there, but *right now*. In this moment, the immediacy, the need, is almost painful.

I move, one foot in front of the other, not fast but with the effort and purpose of someone who *does not want to be*. For a few seconds (that feel like hours) I am caught up in a throng of little ones, crowded outside a bookshop, clinging onto grown up hands, and find myself wanting to scream. If it weren't for the mask, and the strangeness of it, perhaps I would.

Something about their happiness jars with me, but not as much as everything else does. I hate myself for it.

Looking up, the harsh light of the October sky hurts my eyes: dull and yet somehow far too bright. Passing a low-rent version of Kentucky Fried Chicken, I wince without meaning to, just as someone behind you squeezes by, clinking shopping bags bulging with wine, pizzas and beer.

Never one to be a kill-joy, it's not the celebration itself that bothers me, but rather the sheer ordinariness of it. The glaring sign above it all saying – no, shouting – "THIS IS JUST WHAT WE DO," that speaks so palpably, so violently of the life I know I am not living, even though I want to.

In recovery and in life, people talk a lot about bravery, about what it means and what it doesn't. "Recovery is brave," "Doing the next right thing is brave", "Asking for, and accepting help is brave" are phrases I've heard countless times before.

I understand all of this. Of course I do. And in my heart of hearts, I know it's absolutely true. But lately, there's something missing. A disconnect of sorts, somewhere in the deepest corners of my brain.

"Bravery" and "Living" have got lost in translation; two words as hollow and fragile as empty promises, or as loved ones telling me to *just eat.*

It's not new, this feeling of being out of sync, cut off from the rhythm and vibrancy of life. In fact, I know it all too well, often welcoming it in like a long lost friend. Except lately, the familiar numbness has not come alone, having travelled arm-in-arm with sadness, yearning and regret.

Now, more than ever, my past and future selves catch glimpses of something that my current being simply can't. Banging on the window of my mind with all their might, they are begging to be heard, singing the praises of possibility and hoping against hope that one day, I will see it too.

Something that has been so clear to them all along: a version of me bathed and dancing in golden light, living off a joy that is not fleeting or borrowed, but permanent, and absolutely, completely my own.

Chapter 28

The Good Tennant

Yesterday, a doctor asked me some interesting questions.

"If your body were your landlord, how much rent would it charge you for living in its space?"

"And if asked how you've been treating it, what do you think it would say?"

The answers came to me instantly, even before the woman had finished what she was trying to say. As she spoke the words of her final question, my eyes filled with tears, and my cheeks started to redden with what, I think, was shame.

"Are you a good tenant?" she asked, not unkindly, but with a curious, tentative look in her eyes.

Even through my own distorted lens, one thing was clear to me – clearer, perhaps than ever before: I am *not* a good tenant.

But more than just bad, slovenly or even neglectful, I am downright cruel. When it comes to my body, my attitude is that of a tyrant or a despot; someone predisposed to malevolence and hatred.

If my body were my landlord, it would call me out, telling brutal truths of endurance, suffering, punishment and pain, and I would end up living on the streets.

And for what? The pursuit, not of happiness, but of profound, all consuming nothingness. A numbness carefully designed to drown out the din of a harsh and unfamiliar world. A world in which, ultimately, I feel I do not really belong.

Chapter 29

The Epiphany

It's just after 9pm, and I'm sitting on the sofa with a few of the other patients. I couldn't tell you what day it is, since all the days seem to blur into one in this place. All I know is that I feel as though I'm about six months pregnant, and I've had an epiphany.

I'm a bit reluctant to admit to this, because, over the last 13 years, I've had more epiphanies than I have hot dinners (sorry, bad joke), but this time, it feels a bit different. I've just spent the last hour or so chatting with the other girls, and in that time, we seem to have covered everything from how we ended up here (and of course, how much we all want to get out of here), to jobs, children, marriage, the best - and worst - days of our lives, and all of our core beliefs.

A few minutes pass, and suddenly I hear a loud beeping sound coming from somewhere down beside my feet. It's Dave, my feed bag, letting me know that, as far as nutrition goes, I'm done for the day. I breathe a sigh of relief before lifting the bag up, unzipping it, and switching it off.

"Is Dave done?" Natalie asks eagerly.

"Yep. Thank God for that. I just want to throw him out of the window. I'm so done with all of this," I say, blinking away tears.

"Go to the clinic room and get rid of him. Good riddance, Dave! Do you want me to come with you?" she asks, clearly sensing my distress.

"Nah, I'm all good", I say, even though we both know it's a lie. "I'll be back in two minutes, I just need a flush."

"Ok babe. You've got this. See you in a bit."

I make my way to the clinic room, disconnect the feed bag, and dump it unceremoniously onto the floor, before letting the nurse flush my tube with the standard 50ml of water. When I'm done, I take a deep breath and head back to the lounge, doing my best to avoid the temptation of 'bumping' into any walls that I pass on my way.

Sitting back down on the sofa, I turn to Natalie and say triumphantly,

"Nat, don't laugh, but I've had an epiphany."

"Oh my god, really? What is it?" she asks, sounding genuinely excited.

"Well, before I went to the clinic room, I realised something. I've figured it all out!" I tell her enthusiastically.

"Figured all what out?" Natalie asks. Her face is full of curiosity, but I can tell she doesn't know whether to be excited or worried about what I'm going to say.

"Everything," I exclaim, my voice rising as it gathers momentum.

"Everything? She asks again. "Don't tell me you've figured out the meaning of life in the last five minutes. What the hell did they do to you in that clinic room?" she laughs, her eyes shining as she wraps her dressing gown more tightly around her to keep out the evening chill.

"Well, okay, maybe not *everything*. Just *some* things. Mainly, what I need to do to get the hell out of here and live my life," I tell her matter-of-factly, as though it's the simplest and most obvious thing in the world.

"Start eating more?" she asks tentatively, laughing nervously as though she's worried she might have gone too far.

"Well, yeah, obviously that's the first step, but once I'm over that *teeny, tiny* hurdle, I've figured out what I need to do", I say, beaming at her to let her know she hasn't offended me in the slightest.

"LOL! And what's that then?"

"I just need to change all of my core beliefs," I tell her triumphantly, waiting for some sign of approval.

"Right…." Natalie says laughing at me, clearly still not sure whether I'm joking or being serious.

"No, honestly. That's it! That's all I need to do - just take every single one of my core beliefs and throw them in the fucking bin, because really and truly, they're just a load of shit."

"Okay…" she says slowly, trying to work out whether it's okay for her to be finding this funny, or if it's a sign that I'm having some sort of breakdown.

"Because," I continue, by way of an explanation, "almost everything I've ever believed about myself has had something to do with my body, and what I'm eating, or not eating. And it might have taken me 13 years, but now I've realised that none of it fucking matters," I tell her, a huge grin on my face.

"No one cares about how much I weigh, what size my clothes are, how much I've exercised, or whether I've just eaten a 10 course banquet - at least not any of the people I need in my life anyway. It's just that my brain has fixated on all of this as if they're the most important things in the world, when really, they don't count for anything."

"So, to solve the problem, and get the hell out of here, I just need to change all of my core beliefs, and then I'll be good to go," I say proudly, feeling pretty pleased with my revelation.

"You know what," Natalie says, putting a hand on my shoulder and turning to look me straight in the eye, "I actually think you're right. And more than that, I think I need to do the same thing. But the real question is, where do we start?"

"That's the only problem Nat. I haven't got a bloody clue. But you know what Dumbledore says?"

"Of course I don't, you *know* I've never read *Harry Potter*…"

"He says: "Understanding is the first step to acceptance, and only with acceptance can there be recovery". So," I carry on, "we've made the first step,

and that's what counts. Let's just have some diazepam, go to bed, and worry about the rest tomorrow."

Chapter 30

Like a Pig Being Raised for Slaughter

I'm in the MDT room again with Dr Q, but this time we are updating my care plan. In an inpatient unit, each person's care plan is divided into sections: 'Keeping Safe,' 'Keeping Well,' 'Keeping Healthy,' and 'Keeping Connected', all aimed at providing each of us with the right treatment, and ultimately, helping to prepare us to manage our lives out in the real world.

Today, Dr Q is in the process of updating the 'Keeping Safe' section, and after talking at length about my recent episodes of self harm, she asks me if I have anything I would like to add.

I think for a moment, trying my best to come up with something profound and insightful, but nothing springs to mind, so instead, I look her directly in the eye and say in a deadly serious tone:

"I feel like a pig being raised for slaughter."

Dr Q stares at me intently, clearly trying to get a sense of the internal workings of my brain. After an excruciatingly long silence, she says,

"Wow. That's a very powerful statement. It's almost visceral. I don't think I've ever heard anything quite like it. Can you explain what you mean?"

I stare back at her, genuinely surprised that what I said wasn't explanation enough, and reluctantly start to elaborate.

"I *mean,* I feel like a pig. Like I'm just here being force-fed and fattened up ready to be killed and made into packets of sausages or bacon. I feel disgusting. Totally and utterly disgusting."

"Right," Dr Q says slowly, in a way that makes me think she's trying to penetrate right into my soul. "And is there anything we can do to make that feeling a bit less…intense? I'm sure we won't be able to take it away all together, but perhaps you've got something in mind that might help lessen it a little bit, in terms of managing your feelings and keeping yourself safe?"

"Yes," I reply stubbornly. "There is something you can do. Just take this fucking tube out of my face."

"Okay, well I can tell you we aren't going to do that, but it's still important that your voice comes through on your care plan, so how can we word that in a way that's a bit more…politically correct?"

"I don't know," I say with a shrug, feeling a bit like an obstinate child who's being told off in the headteacher's office. "You asked me if I had anything to add, and to explain how I feel, and that's my explanation. I don't know what else to say."

"Right," Dr Q says, obviously getting frustrated with me now. "But if we took out the NG tube, would you follow your meal plan orally? I know you're managing some meals, but would you eat to make up the rest?"

"Absolutely not", I tell her, without a second thought.

"And why is that?" she asks, apparently with genuine intrigue.

"Why?" I say in surprise. Given that we're both sitting in a treatment facility for people who try to eat as little as possible, I'd have thought the answer was obvious.

"Yes. Why don't you want to eat?" she asks again, staring deeply into my eyes.

"Because I can't do it. I never asked for any of this and it's all just being forced on me. I don't want to eat, I don't want to gain weight, and I don't want this tube in my face, but what choice do I have?" I'm shouting now, and my eyes are brimming with tears.

"You *do* have a choice," she tells me emphatically. "You can choose to comply with your meal plan orally, or you can have your nutrition via the NG. At present, those are the two choices you have."

"But both of those amount to the same thing - being force-fed and having to live in a body I can't stand; being forced to have nutrition, one way or the other, when I don't want it. I never signed up for any of this. It's not fair."

"Maybe so," Dr Q says, a little more gently. "But it's also not fair, moral *or* legal, to allow someone to starve themselves to death. And if we took the tube out, you're saying that's what you would do. So, as far as I'm concerned, you're here, and you're not going anywhere until you get the treatment you need, and until you're in a better place - mentally as well as physically."

Sighing inwardly, and doing my best to hold back tears, I stare down at my boots, unsure of what to say. I hate what I'm hearing, almost as much as the situation I'm in, but really and truly, I can't deny that she's absolutely right. If they took the tube out, I wouldn't - I *couldn't* - everything I needed to, and if I left the hospital, things wouldn't be any different. So even though I can hardly bring myself to admit it, the woman's got a very valid point.

Looking up, I see that she's still staring at me, as though I'm some fascinating specimen in a laboratory, and although crying in front of her is the last thing on earth I want to do, I'm unable to stop the tears from streaming down my face.

"So," Dr Q says questioningly, with a sense of finality in her voice. "What shall I write? "Sophia is currently struggling with her meal plan and needs support from the nursing team to comply with feeding via the NG tube?"

"Yeah, I guess that'll do," I tell her reluctantly, trying with all my might to stop myself from making a joke of what is undoubtedly a pretty horrible situation.

As I get up to leave the room, my dark sense of humour gets the better of me, and instead of simply thanking her, I say, "that'll do, pig. That'll do," before closing the door behind me.

Chapter 31

What Would a Whale Do?

"**I** can't do this anymore. I feel like a whale!" I moan to Natalie over WhatsApp, in the 7th voice note we have exchanged that morning, our primary method of communication now that she's been discharged.

"How am I supposed to cope in this body? It's just so unnatural and alien to me. I'm a whale. A huge fucking whale!"

"You're not a whale, you're beautiful, and you're exactly the size you're meant to be," Natalie tells me emphatically.

"You've just been underweight for so long that you've forgotten what it's like to live in a 'normal', healthy body. It might take a while, but you'll get used to it as time goes on, I promise. And if it helps, you're not the only one. I feel like a whale too. I feel like I should be set free to live in the ocean, and not have to go out and get a job and earn money like an ordinary human being. Whales don't have jobs, they just float around in the sea, eating fish and swimming. Why can't I do that?"

Of course, we are joking, but there's a serious side to these messages; one that speaks volumes about how difficult it is to cope with an anorexic mind and anorexic thoughts when you no longer exist in an anorexic body.

And of course, rationally, I *know* I'm not the size of a whale, but that doesn't do anything to change how I feel, and how strongly I want to restrict, simply because that's been my go-to solution for so long.

"Anyway," Natalie continues in her 17 minute long voice note, "I was talking to Janet about all of this in our last session. I told her I feel like a whale, and she told me I'm not but I wasn't having any of it, so in the end, she just said: "well, Natalie, when was the last time you looked at a whale? They're actually really beautiful creatures, and no one judges them for their size. People just take them as they are, and that is how you need to start seeing yourself, too."

Janet is her Eating Disorder Practitioner, and it just so happens that she is mine too, so we tend to compare notes whenever either of us have a session with her. To an outsider, this might seem a little odd, but when you've lived in an EDU with someone for months on end, confidentiality goes right out of the window.

"But yeah, all I'm saying," she goes on, "is that I *think* what we're feeling is normal, for people like us anyway. I think we're going to feel huge when we're so used to living in bodies that have been starved for years and years.

"If it's normal, then why have we spent months and months trapped in a hospital? And more importantly, why does it feel so horrible just to exist? I can't stand being in this body. It's so unbearable -

honestly. I don't know how people do it. How does anyone ever recover?!" I wail into my phone, watching the minutes and seconds clocking up as I speak.

"I get what you mean about it being horrible to exist. I wish I didn't, but I just feel so anxious all the time - especially about going to bed. It's like my body is worrying about where everything goes when I sleep, and I just can't seem to switch off. And lately I've been having a lot of intrusive thoughts. I keep fantasising about death, and plotting different ways to kill myself. I don't think I'd ever do it, but it's kind of scary even having these thoughts. My mum says I should tell Janet about them, but I'm a bit wary of that. I just don't know what she'll say. She'd probably tell me that it's all okay because whales have intrusive thoughts too, they just don't act on them," Natalie says, relishing in her own dark sense of humour.

"Nat, maybe that's it. Maybe you've cracked it", I exclaim with a laugh. "Maybe, whenever we have an intrusive thought, or engage in any 'negative self-talk' or whatever they call it, we should just ask ourselves 'what would a whale do?' It can be the eating disorder version of that Christian slogan that you always see on people's wristbands, except it'd be WWWD instead of WWJD. Basically, whenever we've got a problem, we need to think about it like this: if a whale wouldn't give a shit, then neither should we."

Chapter 32

Girl Boss

D r S is the ward GP, and if I'm honest, I think I'm a little bit obsessed with her. Not in a creepy way, I hasten to add. She's just the kind of person you automatically feel drawn to, even though you can't quite work out why. Maybe it's because of her girl boss vibes, her fashion sense (she always looks especially glamorous on Ward Round days), or because of the way she sings along to Adele at the top of her voice while she takes your bloods, or attaches leads to your wrists, knees, ankles and chest in preparation for an ECG. Either way, she's very cool.

Because she's a GP, she usually has very little to do with the food side of things on the ward, but on one particular day towards the start of my admission, something happened to turn all of that on its head.

For reasons relating to my cerebral palsy, I was unable to move more than a few inches because my legs were in so much pain, so for a period of about four days, I had to have all my meals and snacks in my room. Any normal person would probably think they were living the dream, having all their food served up to them on a tray in bed, but for me, it was an absolute nightmare. Anorexia was having a field day, screaming louder than ever, berating me for being the laziest person alive - in spite of all the pain - and making it almost impossible to eat or drink anything at all. For days, I refused any and all food I was given, only allowing myself to drink tiny sips of water or tea even though my mouth was as dry as a desert. On the third day, when the pain became too much to bear, I agreed to attempt some fruit salad and half a jacket potato, if - and only if - I was allowed to have some stronger pain relief.

When lunchtime came around, there was a knock at my door, and in walked Dr S, carrying a tray with a bowl of fruit salad and a plate covered with a metal cloche.

"Lunchtime!" she said brightly, closing the door behind her and placing the tray down at the end of my bed.

"We're really short-staffed today and there's no one to supervise, so you're stuck with me I'm afraid. I've never supervised a meal before, so I'm kind of winging it, but we've got this. *You've* got this," she tells me, letting out a laugh that's so infectious it's hard to stop myself joining in.

"Where shall we start? The fruit salad is probably easier isn't it? Let's give that a try first," she says, taking the bowl off the tray and handing it to me with a fork and a tablespoon.

"Dr S, I can't", I say pleadingly, hoping that if I look pathetic enough she will take pity on me and just let me get away with having a glass of water.

"You *can*. You've got this, I promise. This is all new territory for me too, but we're in it together."

I stare down at the fruit salad, willing it to disappear, and after only a few seconds, she catches me in the act.

"The more you stare at it, the worse it's going to look. Just pick up the fork and give it a go," she says kindly. "You're doing the right thing, I promise."

I do as she says, hesitating before picking gingerly at the different pieces of fruit as though they're tiny unexploded bombs that might go off at any moment. Spearing a blueberry with the fork, I stare down at it again, putting all my efforts into bringing it up to my mouth, before stopping half way and bursting into tears.

Dr S moves closer, sitting beside me on the bed and putting a hand gently on my shoulder.

"I know it's hard. But I can also see how hard you're trying. You *can* do this," she says encouragingly, smiling from beneath her blue face mask.

"How about you try your best to eat half of what's in that bowl, and for every bite you manage, I'll tell you a funny fact about myself. We'll make it into a bit of a game."

I smile back at her gratefully, wiping away tears with the back of my hand, and agree to give it a proper try.

I pick the fork up again, raise it to my lips, and even though every fibre of my being is willing me not to, I put the blueberry into my mouth and start to chew. Even though I obviously know what blueberries taste like, the flavour sort of catches me off guard. Before being stuck in my room, the only thing I'd eaten since being in hospital was Weetabix, and even that was a struggle, so the taste of something fresh and fruity is a whole new experience; one that feels wrong. So, so, wrong. Like something other people are allowed, but not me.

"Well done! See, you're doing it!" Dr S says enthusiastically. From someone else, this might have come across as patronising, but I can tell she genuinely means it, so I take the encouragement as it's meant, and use it to spur myself on - this time, deciding on a slice of green apple.

"That's it, keep going. You've got this!"

"Wait, you said for every bite I eat you'll tell me a funny fact about yourself. One blueberry equals one fact", I say grinning at her.

"Ah! I was hoping you might forget. I thought I was going to get away with that one," she laughs. "Okay, a funny fact. Let me think…"

She pauses for a moment, pointing at the slice of apple on the fork and motioning for me to make a start.

"Right, I've got one. It's a bit weird, and I'm not sure how many people I've actually told about this, but if nothing else, it *should* give you a laugh. But while I'm telling it, you have to try and have another bite. That's the deal."

Reluctantly I nod in agreement, waiting for the funny fact with baited breath.

"Right, like I said, this is *probably* a bit weird, but I always shower sitting down," she tells me with a giggle.

"Sitting down? Why? How does that even work? I ask, slice of apple poised half way between the bowl and my mouth.

"Well, I must have tried it once for some reason, and ever since then, that's just how I shower. My husband thinks I'm crazy, but I find it so much more comfortable. The ceilings in our flat are a bit low, and I'm quite tall, so it just works better. I even wash my hair like that. I just sort of sit there with the shower on, letting the bath fill up with water, so it's like a half-shower half-bath type thing. I don't even know what you'd call it really."

As she finishes speaking, she lets out the same infectious laugh in a mixture of amusement and embarrassment, pointing as she does so, at my forgotten slice of apple.

"There you go," she says, still giggling. "Now you know something about me that I haven't told any of the other patients. In fact I don't think anyone else knows except my husband. That *definitely* warrants another bite.

Laughing with her, I nod in agreement and begrudgingly take a pathetically small bite of the apple, resisting the urge to pull and pinch at the fat on my body with my fingernails until my skin bleeds and every last bit of it is gone.

"And the rest of it. Come on Soph, you can do this. One more bite and that's another piece gone," she says, her tone firm but still gentle and encouraging.

As I swallow the last piece of apple, tears begin streaming down my face and I push the bowl away from me, having used up what feels like every last resource of strength and effort.

"I'm done Dr S," I say, tears falling thick and fast into my lap, dampening the leopard print fabric of my dress. "I can't take it anymore. I'm just done."

Noting my distress, she puts the bowl back onto the tray and moves it away from me before placing one hand on my shoulder and reaching out for a nearby roll of toilet paper with the other. Handing it to me, she says,

"Here, have some of this. We haven't got any tissues so this will have to do. Wipe those tears and let me run and get some Fortisip. I think that might be easier. I know you've tried, and I commend you for that, I really do, but we've got to get something more in your stomach before I can let you have any more pain relief, or I wouldn't be doing my job properly."

She leaves the room and returns a few minutes later with a cup of vanilla-flavoured Fortisip and a straw, which she hands to me before sitting back down on the bed.

"Right, I've just spoken to the Ward Manager, and she's agreed that if you have two-thirds of this, I'll be able to give you some pain relief. Here, I've even got it with me," she says, opening her fist to reveal a small blister pack containing two raisin-sized pills.

I stare blankly at her, and I feel my whole body tensing up at the mere thought of what I'm about to do. Right now, drinking that fortisip feels about as doable as climbing Mount Kilimanjaro with a blind fold on. In fact, I'd much *rather* climb Mount Kilimanjaro. And then promptly set myself on fire.

As I sit on my bed staring down at the cup of Fortisip, Dr S goes over to my desk and starts rifling through my books, obviously looking for something to read. She stumbles across a pocket-sized collection of arrow word puzzles and begins flicking through them until she finds a fresh page.

"Oooh I've actually never done one of these before. Shall we do it together? I can't promise I'll be any good but we can give it a try", she says, sitting back on my chair, crossing her legs and unclipping a pen from the lanyard around her neck.

"Sorry, I've made myself right at home," she says with the same infectious giggle. "I hope you don't mind!"

"Not at all Dr S, what's mine is yours. Make yourself comfortable. I'll even share my Fortisip with you if you like," I offer, holding out the cup and giving her a wry smile.

"Ha! Nice try Sophia! I can help with distraction as much as you like, but I certainly won't be drinking it for you. Come on, make a start and I'll read some of the clues out as you do it."

Glancing warily from her to the Fortisip and back again, I brace myself and take the first sip. I wince inwardly as the artificial sweetness hits my taste buds, and I half wish I'd stuck with the fruit salad, although deep down I know this will be easier.

"That's it, keep going. You're doing great! I'll give you the first clue and let's see if we can figure it out. And while you're thinking, I want you to have another sip. Ready?"

I nod, despite knowing I've never been less ready for anything in my life, and bring the straw to my lips.

"Okay, the first one is five letters, and the clue is 'Simon _____, singer of the boyband Blue.' Any ideas? I haven't got a clue. I know who he is - I can even see his face - but I've got no idea what his last name is."

"Webbe," I tell her quickly, resisting the urge to break into a terrible rendition of 'Sorry seems to be the hardest word.' "Simon Webbe."

"Ah! Yes, it fits! Okay, have another sip and I'll read out the next clue," she says, nodding in the direction of my cup.

"This one's pretty easy: 'church instrument'. It's got to be organ, right? Yes, it's five letters as well. We need some harder ones or we'll have this done in no time. Keep going, I might be reading this but I've still got my eye on you. Remember our deal - two-thirds of that cup and the pain relief is all yours."

Realising I've got absolutely no choice in the matter, I do as I'm told and take another sip while Dr S reads out the next clue.

"Take small bites, six letters. You should *definitely* know the answer to this one," she says with a laugh. "First letter 'n'.

"Nibble," I say, taking another sip without really thinking too much about it.

"Yes! Okay, we're doing well! Show me. How much have you got left?" she asks, leaning over to peer inside my cup.

"Amazing, a few more sips and you're there. By the time we finish this I reckon you'll be done.

For the next 10 minutes, I carry on drinking the Fortisip while Dr S reads out the rest of the clues, and before I know it, I've finished the agreed quota just as we reach the final clue: 'musical piece for one.'

Handing the cup back to her, I lower my head and break into noiseless sobs that seem to take over my entire body. I know I've done the right thing, but the guilt is so overwhelming I just can't stop myself from crying.

"Hey, hey hey," she says gently, coming back over and sitting beside me on the bed. "Why all the tears? You smashed it. Wipe those eyes and get these down you. Let's get rid of some of that pain, and hopefully you'll start to feel a bit better."

Wiping my eyes with a handful of toilet roll, I take the pain killers from her and swallow them both in one go, grateful that the ordeal is over.

"I know it was hard, but you did it. You should be proud of yourself. And even if you can't be right now, *I'm* proud of you," she says, reaching over to give me a high five.

Next time, we'll see if we can beat our time limit, and if we do, I'll try and come up with some funnier facts about myself, but you have to promise you won't tell *anyone*."

Chapter 33

Uno, But Make It Bollywood

I don't wish to sound dramatic, but today I feel bad. And I mean really, *really* bad. As bad as if I'd told my mum I don't love her, committed a war crime *and* an act of mass homicide all in one day.

If I told you why I feel this way, you'd probably think I was absolutely ridiculous, but if nothing else, that just sums up the horrible, soul-sucking, nonsensical paradox that is anorexia. All I've really done is eaten a tiny, child-sized pot of rice pudding, but I feel like the most terrible person alive, and even *I* - a person *with* an eating disorder - know that doesn't make the slightest bit of sense

Because of how I'm feeling, Paul has predictably made an appearance, having perched himself on my shoulder, perfectly positioned to whisper all manner of terrible 'solutions' into my ear. I should have known it would be coming, because it's at times like this when he tends to strike; on days when I'm at my lowest ebb and feeling the most vulnerable. That's when Paul worms his way into my life.

As always, I do my best not to listen, trying my hardest not to give in to his horrible demands. But on days like today, I feel powerless against him; like a featherweight female boxer heading into the ring with Tyson Fury.

As I finish the last few mouthfuls of rice pudding, the member of staff with me obviously senses my distress and suggests we play a game of Uno, by way of a distraction. Instantly, I decline, politely but firmly, since any form of distraction or enjoyment is an outright violation of Paul's code of conduct. Fun is simply not allowed, and as far as distraction goes, pain is the only option on the table.

But the HCA, whose name is Sonali - isn't having any of it. She knows me well, and has been working on the ward long enough to get a sense of Paul's tricks, and the way he tends to pounce at my weakest moments, particularly following a meal or a snack.

So, she takes me by the hand and leads me out into the garden, picking up a pack of Uno cards along the way.

"Soph, I can see where your head is going but I'm not letting you do this. We are going to play Uno and it's going to be funnnnn. Today we are only letting in positive thoughts. No negativity allowed!" she says enthusiastically, her blue face mask pulled down slightly so that I can see the huge smile on her face.

Reluctantly, I give in and pick up the seven coloured cards she dealt out for me on the table.

"And anyway, you know you're going to win. You *always* beat me. It's my own fault really, I taught you too well!" she says with a laugh.

Sonali turns the first card face up, and we both scrutinise the hands we've been dealt, looking for a card that matches the colour, the number, or both. Before either of us put down our first card, Sonali jumps up from her seat, takes her phone from her back pocket and begins scrolling quickly through her apps.

"It's too quiet out here," she says, opening up Spotify. "What we need is some music to try and distract you from what's going on in your brain. What shall we listen to? Any preferences?"

I shrug, unable to think of a single song that could drown out the cacophony of self-loathing going on in my head, and tell Sonali that she's free to put on whatever music she chooses, since it won't make much difference to me.

"Hmmm…" she says thoughtfully. "Let me think. We need something upbeat but not too noisy, so we can still concentrate on the game, because you know how competitive I get. I know I taught you well, but I still don't like to lose!"

"I know! I'll put on some music we listen to back home. They usually play this song at weddings, and all the people get up and dance, doing the same moves in a…what do you call it? When people all dance together at the same time? Flash something?" She asks.

"Flash mob?" I ask, unsure whether I really know what she's talking about.

"That's it! A flash mob! It's so lovely and romantic, but so, so much fun as well. This is a very popular song where I'm from back in India. We danced to it at my cousin's wedding. I spent aaaages learning all the moves! Are you ready?" she asks, one hand poised over her phone, ready to press play, and the other holding out her cards in a fan shape, carefully hidden from my line of sight.

I nod reluctantly, doubtful that even a combination of Bollywood music and Uno will do much to lighten my mood.

"Okay, let's go!" Sonali says excitedly, pressing play on the song and placing her first two cards down at the same time - a yellow three matching the yellow six that is already on the table, and a green three on top of that.

"Right, your turn," she says pointedly, swaying along to the music, tapping her feet and moving her hands to the jangling beat.

I take my turn, putting down a green five and three more fives on top of that - yellow, blue and red. As I do so, I notice my thoughts start to quieten slightly and in spite of everything, find myself swaying along to the chorus.

"Aha! You're beating me! I *knew* this would happen. You're just too good," Sonali squeals, picking up her phone to find another song to soundtrack our game.

"Any requests or shall I choose again?" she asks. "I didn't know whether you'd like my choice of songs or whether you'd think they were a bit weird."

"No, I actually love them" I tell her with genuine enthusiasm. They're so happy and, like, bouncy. They just make you want to dance."

"Right?! I *told* you we had some really fun songs. I've got the perfect one to finish our game, but for this you *have* to watch the video because their outfits are incredible. Typical dress for Indian weddings, but the colours are *amazing*. Just watch and you'll see.

For the next half an hour, Sonali and I sit in the garden playing Uno and listening to Bollywood music, and for a while, I actually forget where I am. For a few brief moments, I stop thinking about the rice pudding, the NG tube and the feed bag pumping nutrition into my stomach, and allow myself to be transported away from the hospital to a wedding in the bustling, sun-soaked city of Mumbai.

34

For You, When You're Feeling Hopeless

L ately, I've come to realise how powerful positive affirmations can be. Whenever I'm struggling, I repeat the following statements aloud to myself and it usually helps restore a sense of calm, and gets me back on track.

You are safe

You are okay

You are strong

You are brave

You are loved

You are worthy

You can do anything you put your mind to

You deserve happiness

You deserve to rest

You are beautiful

You are joyful

You are courageous

You don't have to be afraid

You don't need to change yourself for anyone

You are in control

Your worth is not affected by what you eat, or how much you exercise

You deserve to be free

You are not alone

You have a lot to offer

You are not a failure

You are not broken

You deserve to enjoy life

It's okay to ask for help

You deserve to take care of yourself

You are enough

You have always been enough.

Chapter 35

Eating a Yoghurt in A&E

I'm sitting in A&E with Nadia, one of the HCAs, and since being triaged, we've been here for almost six hours. To pass the time, both of us are reading books; hers is about female empowerment in relationships, and mine is a short story about a Japanese talking monkey, which probably gives you a bit of an indication as to where my head is currently at.

In case you've not had the misfortune to find yourself in an A&E department for a while, let me set the scene. It's a Sunday, so the place is packed to the rafters. There are screaming children everywhere, lots of people with sporting injuries, and a man in the corner - most likely intoxicated - with a huge gash over his right eye and blood streaming down the side of his face, telling anyone who will listen that he plays the music of Beethoven better than Beethoven himself. Despite having been here for hours on end, with no prospect of being seen by an actual doctor any time soon, I count my blessings and thank my lucky stars that I'm sitting next to Nadia and not blood-spattered Beethoven man who may or may not be very, very drunk.

As much as I don't want to be in A&E, if I could have chosen any member of staff to accompany me, it would have been Nadia. She's been working on the ward for about six months, which in the grand scheme of things, isn't very long at all, but in that time, she and I have been through a lot. She's restrained me more times than I can count, supervised me on the toilet and in the shower, washed my hair, and given me pep talks that rival anything I might have heard from a professional motivational speaker. As HCAs go, she is an absolute gem, and I hope one day she reads this and realises what a huge difference she's made to *all* of our journeys, but in particular, to mine.

As I sit in the hard plastic chair, reading my book about the talking monkey and chugging Pepsi like I've got a train to catch, another half an hour passes and Nadia nudges me on the shoulder, checks the time on her phone and points to a brown paper bag on the floor down by her feet.

"It's snack time darlin'. Shall I get your yoghurt out?" she says, her tone gentle but firm, so I know that what she's asking isn't really a question.

"Nadia I can't. Not in here. There's *so* many people. I just can't do it," I tell her, a pleading look in my eye.

"Mmmm hmmm," she says, shaking her head with a grin, her afro bouncing wildly up and down. "Giiiirl. You have to. You *know* you have to, we're not having no debate about this. And it's not like you're doing it alone. I'm gonna have one with you. I brought one for both of us, and I've been looking forward to it all afternoon. We're doing this together."

SOPHIA PURCELL

"Nadia no! Honestly, I can't. There are so many people in here. I feel like they'll all just stare at me and think I'm really weird," I say, panic rising in my voice. "I mean, who sits in A&E eating a yoghurt?!"

"We do, that's who. Girl, I'm telling you now, no one in this place is gonna stare at you for eating a yoghurt. Take a look around - *so* many people are eating. Look at that little boy over there in the corner," she says with a nod. "He's eating his cookie and absolutely lovin' it. It's written all over his face. And that woman over there, she's eating crisps. There's a man next to her having a sandwich. *Everyone* is eating. It's okay and it's normal. I'm *telling* you. If anyone's looking at us eating our yoghurts, it's because they want them, they're probably hungry."

Looking around me, I realise to my surprise that she's right. Most people around us *are* eating, and if they're not, they look as though they wish they were, if only out of sheer boredom. So, with Nadia's encouragement, I take the spoon, open my yoghurt and reluctantly begin to eat it, spoonful by tiny spoonful, while she sits beside me devouring her own pot in about three mouthfuls, as though it's the most delicious thing in the world.

"Mmmmm hmmm, that was *so* nice. I'm so glad I got to do this with you. I just feel so content right now," she says, putting away her empty yoghurt pot and opening a packet of custard creams with a huge grin on her face.

Meanwhile, I sit ploughing away at my own yoghurt, looking furtively around me as though I'm about to get caught for committing some horrible, terrible crime.

After 10 more minutes, I scrape the last remnants from the pot before handing it back to Nadia, who beams at me and leans in to give me a giant hug.

"Yes girl! You smashed it! You absolutely smashed it. And I know it was hard, but I bet you, I *bet* you, it wasn't as bad as you thought it was gonna be. You built it up in your head, which is totally understandable, but what your head is telling you, none of it is true. You did the right thing, and you are not - I repeat *not* - disgusting. Eating that yoghurt changes absolutely nothing about you. You are still the same smart, creative, beautiful person inside and out, the only difference is you gave your body what it needs, and right now, it's thanking you. I know you might feel disgusting, and like everyone in here is looking at you, but you're not. You're absolutely not. Trust me, because I'm tellin' you the God's honest truth."

While Nadia is talking, I wonder how she's managed to read my thoughts quite so accurately, and I have to fight to stop tears falling from my eyes. I've no idea how, but she just seems to get it, without me even having to say a word, and that is something that hasn't happened to me very often in life. By way of an unspoken thank you, I turn to give her another hug, and as she squeezes me tightly, she whispers, "You did it and you're *not* disgusting. Not even close. I'm so, so proud of you."

As we pull away, I hear the sound of a nurse calling my name, and before we get up to leave, Nadia looks me straight in the eye, in a way that says: "you've got this," and "I meant every single word."

Chapter 36

You Can Do It, Bruce!

"Hola chica! Como estas?"

One of the girls walks up to me and pulls me into a hug. It's warm and comforting, and for a brief moment I forget where I am. I take a deep breath inhaling the strong, flowery scent of her perfume.

This week, she has decided to learn Spanish and so her conversations are peppered with words and phrases that she's got from Duolingo. I kind of like it. It makes things seem much more exotic than they really are. Costa del Psych Ward, as we often say.

"¿Qué pasa Señorita?" She asks again, extricating herself and wrapping one arm around my shoulder.

"Ah, I don't know. I'm just stressing about dinner I think."

She nods, and gives me a knowing look, as though we've reached an unspoken understanding.

"The pudding? Have you gone for the..."

"The Bakewell tart?" I say, finishing the sentence off for her.

"Yep. And now I can't think about anything else, even though it's only 10am. How ridiculous is that?"

"No, it's not ridiculous. Don't beat yourself up. You have every right to be feeling the way you are. And I know you're not the only one. Is it anything in particular that's worrying you, or just the whole shabang?"

"Well, we've had it before haven't we? A few weeks ago. And the portion was insane. It was just so big. Last time I actually ran out of the dining room."

"Hmm...you're not wrong. It was pretty meaty. Well not meaty. More...Bakewell-y. You know what I mean. It didn't even fit in the bowl properly did it?"

I shake my head in agreement, having to make a conscious effort to stop myself from wincing.

"Just think, every bite brings us one step closer to getting out of here, and one step closer to achieving our dreams. For me, that's getting a bum like JLO's. Who doesn't love a little junk in the trunk?"

We both laugh.

"And boobs," I say. "I've actually forgotten what it feels like to have boobs." I raise a hand to my chest and she does the same, both of us imagining how it would feel to have a proper bust instead of almost nothing at all.

"Totally! Me too. Who wants to look like an ironing board? I know I don't. Plus, new boobs are the perfect excuse to buy new underwear." Her eyes light up, and I can tell at once that her mind is elsewhere. No longer on the stuffy ward of a psychiatric hospital, but caught up in the bustle of Oxford Circus or Piccadilly, perusing the shelves of Victoria's Secret, Boux Avenue, and Agent Provocateur.

After a moment or two, her expression changes again, and she looks a little lost, frightened even, as though, even in her imagination this is all a bit too much to handle.

"But, anyway," she says brightly. "Tonight. The Bakewell tart. I've got it too; I think most of us have, so we're all in this together. It'll be like that bit from *Matilda* with the massive chocolate cake. Have you seen it?"

Her face widens into a wicked grin, and as I realise what she's talking about, mine does too.

"You know, the bit where that boy has to go up on stage and eat that humongous cake in front of the whole school? And in the end, when he's flagging and it looks like he's about to throw up, all the other kids start chanting, 'You can do it, Bruce!'"

"That'll be us tonight," she says, beaming at me.

Hours later, when dinner time has rolled around again, we are all in the kitchen sitting down to eat. At the end of the main meal, one of the staff reaches into the hotplate and hands out the bowls of Bakewell tart, each one finished with a scoop of vanilla ice cream. To most people, these puddings would be unremarkable - nothing either good or bad, just something warm and sweet, to be enjoyed and then quickly forgotten. But to us, they are more than that. Something to be feared, but also, once eaten, something to be proud of. A symbol of triumph, and perhaps, of hope. Of bad days behind us, of better days to come. And of course, boobs.

As I pick up the spoon, the girl catches my eye, raises her fist in the air and says, "You can do it, Bruce!"

Chapter 37

Material Girl on a Broke Girl's Budget

To most people, a trip to Nandos probably sounds like something enticing - a treat, even. But for someone with an eating disorder, it is nothing short of terrifying. This might seem a tad dramatic, but really and truly, there have been many points in my life when, thanks to anorexia, I'd have rather gouged out my own eyeballs than spent the afternoon eating in Nandos, or any other restaurant for that matter. So, I'm sure it's going to sound a little bit crazy when I say that this week I actually *asked* to put myself through that ordeal, and that I did so *voluntarily,* even going as far as requesting the day leave during

Ward Round, and sitting down with the dietician to discuss which options from the menu would match up with my meal plan. If you asked me why I did it, even now, I couldn't really tell you. It wasn't long after Dr Hilary had been on *Good Morning Britain* talking about calories being listed on menus, telling the nation that it didn't really matter anyway because "people with eating disorders don't eat out in restaurants." Spurred on by pure rage, I think I just threw caution to the wind and had a bit of a 'fuck it' moment, which, after spending 13 long years being ruled by anorexia, is something I'm pretty proud of.

In saying this, I don't mean to imply that this was a decision I entered into lightly. In actual fact, it required weeks of painstaking deliberation and planning - firstly which restaurant to go to, and secondly, what to order. With half of my nutrition still coming via the NG tube, this wasn't really something I *wanted* to do, but rather, something I felt I *had* to do. I'd been in hospital long enough that the time had come for a challenge, and after much umming and ahhing, I decided Nandos would be it.

The Consultant approved my leave, although I think even she was a little taken aback, and once I'd been given the green light, my only remaining task was to choose which member of staff I wanted to accompany me, since I still wasn't allowed to leave the hospital unescorted. For me, this was the easy bit. I knew exactly who I wanted by my side - so much so that I didn't even have to think twice.

"Amanda! Guess what?! We're going to Nandos!" I exclaimed as I left the MDT room, filled with a mixture of half excitement, half terror.

"YES GIIIIIRRRLLL!" Amanda squeals back at me, flicking back her long red braids. "When's the big day?"

"Wednesday. I've got leave from 12-4pm and I've gone through the menu with Janet to make sure she's okay with what I'm having."

"Ahhh, I'm so excited," she says, a huge smile lighting up her whole face. "How are you feeling about it?"

"Honestly, right now, I don't think I've ever been more scared of anything in my entire life. I sort of can't believe I'm doing it," I say, a slight tremor in my voice.

"But you know you have to, right? Doing things like this is the only way you're ever gonna get your ass outta here, and anyway, it's you and me. You *know* we gonna have fun! You don't need to be scared. I've got you baby girl."

Like many of the staff on the ward, Amanda and I have been through a lot. But for every bad moment we've had, there's been a positive one that far outweighs the rest. Like the time she bought us all matching Christmas jumpers to wear on Christmas Jumper Day, when she held my hand as I sobbed my way through every bolus feed whenever she was on shift, spent hours braiding my hair, or took me out for an iced coffee and some meditation in the sun, or even - and possibly best of all - when she helped another patient wax my legs in the middle of the lounge on Christmas Day.

So, when the time came to choose my Nandos buddy, I *knew* it had to be Amanda.

When the big day arrives, we get out of the taxi by the shopping centre, and head in the direction of the big red 'Nandos' sign just across the road. By this point, I'm shaking so much that I have to use every ounce of strength not to fall flat on my face outside the restaurant, but Amanda takes my hand, motions for me to take a few long, deep breaths, and says,

"Girl, breeeeatheee. It's okay. You've got this. Just take things one step at a time, and if it all gets too much we don't have to stay. We'll go at your pace. Just breathe."

We go inside and wait to be seated, and all the while I'm conscious that I must look very out of place. Not only am I clearly on the verge of a panic attack, but I've got an NG tube in and a rucksack full of feed on my back. Glancing around at all the people happily enjoying their meals, I notice how 'normal' eating seems here, and what a contrast the atmosphere is to any mealtime back on the ward. Here, food is something to be savoured and enjoyed, not dreaded and sobbed over. I can't help but feel a pang of envy somewhere inside me, and I wonder if I'll ever get to a place like that, where the act of eating is as ordinary and commonplace as breathing, not served up with a big dollop of guilt.

We take our seats and I stare down at the menu, scanning it for the one dish I've agreed on with the dietician and 'allowed' myself to have.

After a few seconds, Amanda catches me lingering over the side dishes and says firmly,

"I know the calories are there, but just try to forget about them. Choose what you're having and then I'll get rid of the menus so you don't have to look at them anymore."

We place our order on the app and as we wait, I sit silently praying that someone will come over to tell us that they haven't got any of the right ingredients in stock so we'll have to go somewhere else. Unsurprisingly, that doesn't happen, and after a few minutes our food arrives - Amanda's half chicken and two sides, and my rainbow bowl with halloumi.

I stare down at it blindly, as though I've never seen a plate of food before in my life, and Amanda picks up her knife and fork, motioning for me to make a start too.

"Amanda, I can't," I say weakly. "I thought I could do this, but it's just too much. I feel like my head is going to explode."

"Girl, you *can*. You can and you will. You're stronger than you give yourself credit for. Just pick up that knife and fork and give it a go. You don't have to finish it all if you can't manage it, all you have to do is try your best. Even setting foot in here is a massive step."

I do as I'm told, and it's not until I pick up the cutlery that I notice how much my hands are shaking. Taking a deep breath, I spear the first mouthful with the fork and raise it to my lips, and all the while, Amanda is willing me on from across the table. She doesn't speak - probably because she's worried it will disturb my momentum - but her eyes are saying, "yes girl! Keep going!"

As is often the case, after the first mouthful, I manage to focus on the taste of the food, rather than what it represents, or the mixture of fear and adrenaline that's coursing through my body, and the whole ordeal doesn't seem quite as bad. So, with Amanda's encouragement, I keep going, doing my best to block out the noise of the anorexic thoughts in my head, until I've eaten just over half of what was on the plate. At this point, I know I've reached my limit, so I set my knife and fork down together and let out a long, slow breath.

"See!" Amanda exclaims, her eyes full of genuine pride and happiness. "You smashed it. I knew you would!"

I smile back at her, wishing I could feel just the tiniest amount of pride myself, instead of the horrible concoction of guilt and shame so intense that it's almost eating me alive.

"I know you don't feel good, but I'm really bloody proud of you. You tried *so* hard. Come on, let's go get you some retail therapy. Best form of distraction. Don't let me spend too much money though, it's too far away from payday and I'm a material girl on a broke girl's budget."

Chapter 38

"I'm Bringing the Ginger"

Before dinner, a few of us are in the lounge playing our third game of Rummikub, and to put it mildly, things are getting tense. In case you've never played it, I'll give you a brief run-down of how it works. Each person selects 14 tiles at random and places them on a rack in front of them, hidden from all the other players. The object of the game is to be the first person to place all their tiles on the table, either consecutively (the tiles are numbered from one to 13 and the numbers are either red, yellow, black or blue), or in groups of the same number.

The rules state that in order to play your first go, the tiles you lay down must add up to at least 30 - for example 11,11,11; 8, 9, 10, 11, 12, 13 and so on - and as things stand, all of us have played except one member of staff - Orla. As each of us continue to play our turn, this time adding just one or more tiles to the ones already on the table as per the rulebook, she sits there picking up tile after tile, still unable to reach the minimum required amount, and from the look on her face, the frustration is clearly mounting. When her turn comes round again, she stares at the numbers on her rack, doing some frantic mental maths and trying to work out whether any combination of her fastly growing collection of tiles adds up to 30. When it doesn't, she grimaces, and reluctantly leans over to pick up yet another tile, which she has to place on the table beside her because there's no space left on the rack.

At first glance, Rummikub seems like a relatively simple - and arguably pointless - number game, but when you're locked in a hospital 24 hours a day with little else to occupy your time, it's actually serious business. At this point, I play it on average about 5 times a day, so I'm getting pretty good (even if I do say so myself), and although I wouldn't say I'm a very competitive person, when it comes to Rummikub, it's a whole different story. I just want to win. Not because I like winning, and not even because I particularly like Rummikub. I want to win because it gives me a brief moment of peace and contentment away from the anorexia, and the relentless barrage of noise and insults that is always going on inside my brain.

I lay down three 10s straight off, and after my second go, only have 7 of the 14 tiles left on my rack, so as it stands, my chances are looking good - especially when you consider the fact that one person hasn't even had their first turn.

After yet another round of being unable to play, the rest of us offer to look at Orla's tiles in an attempt to help her out, to see if there's any way of successfully matching the colours and numbers to get to a total of 30. But try as we might, it's no good. Orla really has picked the most random - and unfortunate - selection of numbers, and there's just no way of reaching 30 with the tiles she has.

After a few more rounds, just when we're all starting to think she has no chance of playing at all, Orla jumps to her feet, and with a flick of her hand, exclaims, "YES! You all better watch out. I'm bringing the ginger!"

"You're bringing the what?" the rest of us ask in unison, beginning to wonder whether staring at all these numbers has confused her brain to the point of incomprehension.

"The ginger!," She squeals excitedly, still jumping up and down. "I'm bringing the ginger!"

"Orla, I don't get it, what does that even mean? I've never even heard that phrase before. Have you just made it up?" I ask with a sceptical laugh.

"It's a Nigerian phrase," she says grinning at me. "People say it all the time back home. It means like…how do I describe it? It means…I'm *ready.* I'm *comin'.* I've *arrived.* Watch *out*!"

And with that, she picks up 9 tiles and places them down on the table all at once.

"Boom!" she shouts, snapping her fingers in the air again.

"Ah, Ola! Here we all were thinking you'd never be able to play, and now you're just gonna sweep in and claim your victory at the last minute!" fixing her with a sideways grin.

"Yessss!" she replies enthusiastically, "I might have taken my sweet time, but now I'm gonna win and there's nothing y'all can do about it."

"Hey, hey, hey, me and Leila only have two tiles left, and you've still got five to go. It's not over yet Orla", I tell her, pretending to be much more annoyed than I really am. In actual fact, seeing the look on her face knowing that she's managed to catch up with us is giving me much more enjoyment than winning the game ever could.

"You just wait. I'm just waiting on one last tile and this *whole* game is mine!" Orla says playfully.

"Hmmm," Leila says with a sneaky look in her eye. "You're making me not want to put anything down just to stop you from winning. I'm going to keep picking up tile after tile so you have to do the same."

"Leila, you can't. That's cheating!" Orla says defiantly, reaching out to pick up another tile.

"It's not cheating. It's called being strategic - there's a big difference", Leila says with a smirk.

"Well, I don't care what you say, *I* call it cheating. You can't just not put anything down just to stop me from winning. That's not fair! Plus if you do that we'll just keep going until all the tiles are gone and none of us will win!"

"As much as I don't want Ola to win, I'm going to play my turn because I've only got two tiles left and I reckon I've got a good chance of beating you *all*," I say, placing my penultimate tile - a red eight - down in front of a 9, 10 and 11.

As I do so, Ola squeals and flicks her fingers again, before moving my tiles to make room for her winning move: 3, 4, 5, 6 and 7.

"Mmm hmmm!" she says, slamming her empty rack down triumphantly and jumping up from her seat again, this time to do a little victory lap of the lounge. "I *told* you I was bringing the ginger. I'm the new EDU Rummikub champion. I don't think I've ever felt prouder in my life!"

"Well played Ola, well played," Leila says, picking up her remaining tiles and putting them back in the box.

As much as neither of us wanted Ola to win, it's impossible to deny how good it felt to have some respite from our thoughts, even for just a short while. We may not have a magic wand, or be able to make any huge changes in our recovery overnight, but it's at times like this when I realise how powerful distraction - and learning a new phrase - can be.

Chapter 39

"I'm Not Sunshine, I'm Thunder!"

I'm in breakfast supervision drifting off to sleep, when all of a sudden I hear the sound of an alarm going off somewhere down the corridor. Although this isn't unusual, I'm slightly surprised, because looking around the room, I see that two of the regular culprits - myself included - are sitting peacefully in the lounge. By process of elimination, I work out that the alarm must have been pulled for Suzi, and when I realise what time it is, my heart sinks.

As much as the sound of the alarm can be startling, it never bothers me on a personal level. Whenever the noise starts up, I just feel sad for whoever is struggling, and more than anything, I wish I could do something to help them, even though I know that's totally impossible.

After a while, I hear the sound of doors being forced open, banging on their hinges, as staff from the wards downstairs - reinforcements - come up to assist. Although I can't see anyone from where I'm sitting, I can tell from the sound of the footsteps that there must be a lot of them, which makes sense, because poor Suzi has been having a particularly tough few days. If anything, I really ought to have predicted this, but I suppose, as always, I was hoping for the best.

Nobody *wants* to be restrained. I know this only too well, having had many unfortunate and distressing experiences myself. But on days when the anorexia is particularly strong, you really are fighting a losing battle, and nothing anyone says or does will make the slightest bit of difference. Even so, I sit bolt upright in my chair, ears pricked for any sounds of debate or conversation, hoping against hope that the worst won't have to happen, and maybe - just maybe -

things will be different this time. But after a few moments, my hopes are dashed, as I watch one member of staff run out of the clinic room shouting for someone to call the doctor and get the bean bag, which, if you've ever been to an EDU yourself, you'll know is *never* a good sign. Bean bag equals restraint, and calling the doctor equals the NG tube - both of which really are as unpleasant as they sound. Like I say, *nobody* wants to be restrained, to have six or seven burly men hold you down with a bean bag covering your legs, pulling your head back while a doctor forcibly inserts a tube up your nose and down your throat. And obviously things like this are never entered into lightly; they only ever happen as a last resort, when every other option has been exhausted.

After a while, the alarm ceases, only to be replaced by screaming and shouting so loud you'd think someone was being murdered.

"Get your hands OFF me! I'm not having it. I've already told you I'm not having it. Don't do this. Just get your fucking hands off me - PLEASE! I can't do this anymore. It's not fair. I don't want it. Please just leave me alone," Suzi shouts.

Next I hear one of the staff, voice raised to make herself heard over all the noise, trying her damndest to de-escalate the situation.

"Come on sunshine, you know we have to do this, and we're only doing what's best for you. You need to have your feed, and if you're going to keep pulling the tube out, this is the only way. Please try to calm down, you don't want to make this any harder than it already is."

"DON'T CALL ME SUNSHINE! I'M NOT SUNSHINE, I'M THUNDER!" Suzi shouts, even louder than before.

All of a sudden, the shouting stops, and from inside the clinic room, comes the sound of what - I think - must be laughter. And not just giggling, but proper belly laughs, the kind that shake you from your head, right down to your toes. But it can't be. It doesn't make sense. Less than two minutes ago Suzi was shouting, screaming and swearing, held down by staff and on the brink of being force-fed by bolus, and now she's laughing - they're *all* laughing, as though they're having the time of their lives. "What the hell is going on in there?" I think, more confused now than ever. "What can they possibly be laughing about?"

A few minutes pass, and Suzi comes out of the clinic room, her face red from crying - and apparently - from laughing, NG tube firmly in place, but in spite of it all, and to my complete surprise, she is smiling, walking down the corridor arm in arm with the staff.

"I'm sorry Suz," one of them says, still in a fit of giggles. "I know it's not a laughing matter, but I just couldn't keep a straight face - none of us could. That was the last thing I expected you to come out with. We won't be calling you Suzi anymore. Now you'll be known as 'Little Miss Thunder' right up until the day you're discharged."

Chapter 40

Coming Home

"look down at your body
whisper,
There is no home like you
thank you"
– Rupi Kaur

For as long as I can remember, I've always felt at
odds with myself. As a small child, I knew I was
different, but it was a long time before I really
understood what that meant.

At first glance, my body looked just the same as
everyone else's. I had the 'right' amount of
everything: two arms, two legs, ten fingers, ten toes,

and all the bits in between. On the inside, too, I ticked all the relevant boxes: heart? Check. Lungs? Check. Liver? Kidneys? Check. Check.

Still, deep down I had this sense that something was different; a bit out of sync. There were things other people's bodies could do that mine couldn't; things other people found easy that, for me, were a struggle; things I watched those around me do every day that I found downright impossible. For a long time, I didn't understand why. All I knew is that I was angry. Very, very angry.

Growing up, I was just like most other children. I wanted to do the same things, wear the same clothes, and play the same games as everybody else. More than anything, I wanted to fit in.

The older I got, the stronger these feelings got. Instead of growing into myself and accepting my body for what it was, I became more and more frustrated. I began to resent it. Even on the good days, I saw it as something that made things more difficult than they needed to be. To me, my body was a nuisance, a hindrance; something that got in the way.

If our bodies are the vessels through which we experience the world, mine felt broken, full of cracks and faults and holes, many of them invisible to the naked eye. Not a gift, and not perhaps a curse, but certainly a barrier. A shining beacon of difference. A potent reminder of everything I wasn't, and everything I'd never be.

At school, these feelings of being 'not quite right' were amplified, turned up to full volume. Caught up in an ableist system that revolves around measurement and comparison, I felt more trapped than ever.

While other children were frightened of ghosts and monsters under the bed, my biggest fear was finding out that my best wasn't enough. That somehow, *I* wasn't enough. For me this was the stuff of nightmares, and in the classroom, it was something I was forced to confront on a daily - sometimes hourly - basis.

Academically I was fine. In many areas I excelled, but even so, everything I did felt tainted. Nothing existed in and of itself; every achievement had a caveat. Normal things were often seen as remarkable, and if I did well, it was in spite of the context, in spite of the circumstances, in spite of myself.

Outside of school, the measurement and comparison continued. For years, my life was punctuated by hospital appointments, medical assessments and surgeries. I was prodded and poked and analysed and tested, and although at first I quite liked having time off school, the novelty soon wore very thin. I spent my days trying as hard as I could to keep up, to conform to a mould that I simply didn't fit. It was exhausting.

Held up against some unachievable, universal standard, every appointment was an indication of difference. Every procedure a reminder that I did not fit the space

marked 'child.' The outlines were there, but inside, things weren't quite as they were supposed to be. Some areas were left blank, while others were coloured in messily, haphazardly, in a wobbly, jarring scrawl.

Language is how we make sense of things. It is how we communicate, and how we come to understand ourselves and the world around us. It is also how I came to believe that my body was, somehow, wrong.

With every hospital visit, I was exposed to a whole new world of vocabulary. Alongside the obvious medical jargon, there was correctional language, too. Words like 'fixing', 'correcting', 'normal', 'impairment', 'proper'. Words like 'disabled.' As much as I might try to avoid it, the evidence was there, unequivocally. The failure of my body writ large for all to see.

It was during this time that I also came to associate my body with pain. Not only did it need to be corrected, but it caused me suffering in the process.

Instead of treating it with kindness, thanking it for all it had endured, the resentment I felt towards my body grew even more. For as long as I could remember, it had been letting me down, and for that, it deserved to be punished.

Didn't it?

I've been asking myself that question ever since I was a child, and only now, after years of trying to destroy it, do I know the answer:

My body is not the problem. It never was. My body may not be perfect, but it doesn't have to be. My body is my home. It is the only home I will ever have. My body is enough. *It has always been, enough.*

Chapter 41

The Decline and Fall of Paul and Dave

I f you've seen the film *Love Actually,* you'll probably remember that scene where the guy who's in love with Kiera Knightley turns up at her house to declare his undying love to her. He's got a boom box and those huge flashcards, and 'Silent Night' is blaring away in the background. And at the end of it all, he walks away, looks at the camera and quietly says, "enough. Enough now." That's what it was like for me, getting rid of Paul and Dave. I knew they were doing me more harm than good, and finally, it was time for them to go.

I'm not sure how or why it happened, but I just woke up one morning and decided that enough was enough. I know it won't be like that for everyone (I never, *ever* dreamed it would happen for me), but one day, something just 'clicked.' In saying this, I don't mean that my eating disorder just disappeared. If anything, the voices inside my head got louder and more insistent, screaming at me for disobeying them, for *choosing* to eat instead of being fed through a tube, and *choosing* not to start my day by causing myself harm. But the louder they got, the more determined I became. I didn't *want* to eat anymore than I did on the day I was first admitted, and my self harm urges hadn't gotten any less intrusive or powerful. But nevertheless, something had changed. More than anything, I wanted to get out of hospital, and I knew that the only way out was to eat. It almost felt as though I'd finally found the golden ticket, when in reality, all that had happened was that I'd realised the only way out was through. *Through* the anguish, and through the pain. Eating, even though I didn't want to, *not* self-harming even though Paul wanted me to, and doing everything I could to get myself to a better place, both mentally and physically.

Day by day, hour by hour, I began to learn the true power of distraction, occupying my time with art therapy, reading, studying and games, instead of destructive, self-sabotaging coping mechanisms. Things didn't always go in my favour, but I was trying, and it wasn't long before all my hard work was rewarded.

With the help of the Consultant and the MDT, I started to set weekly goals for myself; incentives for not giving into Paul's demands, or for challenging myself to have dinner instead of relying on Dave for my nutrition. If I managed it, I was allowed home leave, time off the unit, and to join in on ward trips or to go into the local town for a cup of proper coffee - which, after months and months of instant decaf, was a little slice of heaven.

Slowly but surely, I began to feel more and more like myself - the *real* me that exists underneath the distorted veil of anorexia - and I allowed myself to believe that real, full recovery was possible, rather than some sort of 'pipe dream' that could happen for other people but not me.

Everyone - myself included - was bowled over by the transformation I'd undergone.

"It's like Sophia 2.0!", one of the other patients exclaimed as we sat in supervision chatting and discussing our plans for weekend home leave.

"Honestly," she said, her eyes shining and bright, "I really do feel like I'm meeting you again for the first time. You're almost like a different person now!"

"It's true", chimes in Nadia, the HCA who sat in A&E with me eating a yoghurt. It's like you've been in hibernation, and now you're finally starting to blossom. It's so beautiful to watch."

"What's your secret?" someone else asks me with a grin. "Whatever you've done, I want to do it too!"

"Honestly, I've got absolutely no idea," I say, looking around the room to see all the other patients beaming back at me.

"I guess I've just realised that we only get one life, and this awful illness has already stolen enough of mine -

of all of ours. I've decided it's time to start living the life I actually want to live. And to do that, I think I've finally accepted that I have to eat. And also, it might sound stupid, but food is *nice*, isn't it? If we're all *really* honest with ourselves, we've got to admit that food is bloody delicious, and if other people can have it and enjoy it, surely we can, too. I know I was scared out of my wits, but going for that Nandos the other day gave me a glimpse of what 'normal' life *could* be like, and I want more of that!"

As I finish my little speech, everyone in the room starts clapping and cheering, as if we'd come to the end of some sort of TED talk, and as the excitement dies down, I can't help but feel a bit embarrassed. I'm not used to having so much attention on me and it feels unnatural.

"Soph, I'm *so* proud of you," says Lucy, one of my closest friends on the ward. "You've come such a long way in the time I've known you, and it won't be long before you can go out and live the life you truly deserve."

I feel my cheeks redden as she speaks, and in spite of the embarrassment, I can't help but smile.

"That's the thing though Luce," I tell her emphatically. "It's not just me. I bet there were times when *none* of you ever thought I could turn things around - I know I thought that. But I have, and I am, and if I can do it, all of you can do it, too. It might feel impossible at times, but none of us are alone in this, we're all in it together. We just have to keep fighting."

Epilogue
Golden Seams

"And when you tap into hope's golden seams,
you will find the most precious thing of all.
You will find that it is unbreakable."
– Elizabeth Day

If I've learned one thing from my inpatient experiences, it would be this: no matter what you are going through, and no matter how dark things may seem, there is always hope. As you will have gathered from reading these pages, there have been many times when I believed that all hope was lost, and that despite all the support I had around me, there was no way I would ever experience any kind of peace. Now, several months after being discharged from my second admission, I know that this isn't true. There is no magic wand (oh, how I wish there was), but there is a lot to be said for perseverance, the kindness of strangers, and the determination to never give up. Even when it all feels like an uphill struggle and you have nowhere to turn, there is always a glimmer of hope and a reason to keep going. As well as friends, family and of course the staff in the hospital, for me, this came in the probably slightly unorthodox form of a diploma in counselling, a course I enrolled on shortly before I was admitted to an EDU and placed on a Section 3 for the second time. Throughout my admission, this course was one of the main things that kept me going, even during the darkest moments. It gave me something to aim for, a sense of purpose, and an identity that had nothing at all to do with my eating disorder, but more than anything, it gave me hope. Hope for the future, and for brighter days ahead. So, all I can say is that if you're out there experiencing something similar, please, please don't give up. Keep going, keep fighting, and keep looking for the little things that make life that bit brighter. Because no matter how bad things may seem, there is always, *always* hope.

Resources

Here are some resources you might find helpful if you or someone you love is struggling with an eating disorder. The list is by no means exhaustive, but these are just some of the things that have helped me through the darkest of times

Websites

Beat - www.beateatingdisorders.org.uk

Mind - www.mind.org.uk

Rethink Mental Illness - www.rethink.org.uk

Samaritans - www.samaritans.org.uk / 116 123

Shout - www.giveusashout.org.uk / 85258

NHS - https://www.nhs.uk/mental-health/feelings-symptoms-behaviours/behaviours/eating-disorders/overview/

My blog - www.pinksparklybeads.wordpress.com

Books and poems

The Butterfly Effect -

"You need to stay. And you need to stay loudly. You're afraid of making bad choices but the truth is this: the tiniest actions will influence the course of the rest of your life and you cannot control it.

So many factors play a part in you being here today: a delayed train, an extra cup of tea, the number of seconds your parents took to cross the street. This is chaos theory. Sensitivity. Mathematics. You are here. And every choice you ever made has led to right now, reading this. While you exist, every movement and moment matters; those bad choices led you to the best days of your life, if you were to play it all in rewind. So let them go.

Change will come. Even if you're standing still. Butterflies will keep flapping their wings and causing hurricanes. So, make your choices and make them loud. Trust your gut. Trust energy. And if you ceased to exist? Oh the Universe would notice. The mess that would make. The hearts that would break. So just stay.

Stay for bad choices. Stay for great ones. Stay. Cause a few hurricanes."

    – S.R.W Poetry

The comfort book, Matt Haig

Reasons to stay alive, Matt Haig

The boy, the mole, the fox and the horse, Charlie Makesy

Weight expectations, Dave Chawner

Home Body, Rupi Kaur

The book of hope, Johnny Benjamin

Serious concerns, Wendy Cope

Dream work, Mary Oliver

Printed in Great Britain
by Amazon